THE MYSTERY AND PRINCIPLES OF BIBLICAL TITHING

CHARLES LAMPTEY

FIRST EDITION: COPYRIGHT © CHARLES LAMPTEY 2005
Second Edition: Copyright © CHARLES LAMPTEY 2009

All rights reserved. No part of this publication may be reproduced, stored in a retrieval system or transmitted in any form or by any means, electronic, photocopying, recording or otherwise, without the prior permission of the publisher.

"Ask and it will be given to you."

Requests for information should be addressed to

The Administrator

The LAMPS PUBLICATIONS

E-mail: Lamptey@fountain-gate-chapel.de

Scripture quotations are from the New International Version of the Bible (Copyright © 1984 by International Bible Society) unless otherwise indicated.

Cover-Design by Kingdom Design, Tel: 0049 (0)421 420 029

DEDICATION

To my dear wife Carola Lamptey for her great achievement in typing and typesetting the complete manuscript of this book.

CONTENTS

ACKNOWLEDGEMENTS 6

PREFACE 8

F O R E W O R D 10

INTRODUCTION 12

THE CONCEPTS OF COVENANT AND GIVING 27

TITHES AND TAXES 54

THE INSTITUTION OF TITHING 63

WHY GOD HAS INSTITUTED TITHES 68

WHERE WE ARE TO BRING THE TITHE 72

THE RECIPIENTS OF THE TITHE AND ITS USE 81

THE CONSEQUENCES OF ABSTAINING FROM TITHING 95

GOD'S PROMISES TO FAITHFUL TITHERS 103

THE NEGATIVE RESULTS OF FAILING TO TITHE ... 113

THE FORM OF THE CURSE IN THE SPIRITUAL REALM 124

TAKING THE BLESSING BY FAITH 138

IN TITHES AND OFFERINGS 147

THE GENEROSITY OF THE EARLY CHURCH 155

HINDRANCES TO TITHING 162

IMPORTANT FACTORS INVOLVED IN TRUE TITHING 173

THE ELEVEN PRINCIPAL STEPS TOWARDS SAFE TITHING 182

PROBING QUESTIONS ON, WHY BE RICH? 186

ACKNOWLEDGEMENTS

This book has taken more than a decade to prepare and to write, and many people encouraged me during the entire process. However, with much persistence and keen focus, it has finally been birthed to the glory of our glorious, great and glorified GOD. Hallelujah!

I want to acknowledge everyone who participated in the writing of this book for their help and support, without which this project would never have been accomplished.

Nothing in life is ever successful without the corporate effort of many gifted people who are willing to network and submit their talent, experience and passion for a common goal. Dr. Myles Munroe puts it this way, **"We are the sum total of all the people we have known, met and learned from."**

The exposure of the knowledge placed in this book is a result of the prayer, faith and love of many individuals whose trust and commitment to God challenged me to encourage others.

I thank God for the privilege to write in His name. May He be magnified and glorified forever!

I also wish to thank my ministerial mentor, the late Pastor Werner Gunia for his relentless effort to cross check the details of this book. May the Lord bless you and your entire family.

To Leslie Richford, my excellent editorial advisior and guide in developing this manuscript. You are an author's dream and a gift to many who will read this book. Thank you for your great assistance.

To Rev. Eastwood Anaba, my spiritual mentor, whose initial advice and remarks stretched my faith to face the "unknown" without fear. The Lord richly bless you.

My sincere thanks and appreciation also go to Dr. Chege Kamau and his wife, Victoria Chege for additional editorial work. Your effort shall not be forgotten.

To all the congregation and leaders of our ministry in Bremen and in Bremerhaven – Germany – thank you for allowing me to develop and refine these ideas and concepts as I shared and tested them with you. May the windows of heaven forever be opened to you!

Preface

The Biblical subject of tithing is quite delicate and controversial especially to the "New Wine Christian" (i.e. the contemporary Christian). However, it leaves no room for any saint to rebel against its authenticity and virtue.

Arguments such as to whether tithing is still valid in our time, should not be a bothering issue for the New Testament Christian, especially for those who sincerely love God with all their heart. Thus, when it comes to the subject of tithing in our time, the sophists, with their clever but invalid arguments, must be ignored. The tithe is vividly described in the holy Bible as "... holy to the Lord" (cf. Lev. 27:30).

The contemporary Christian is not required to practise tithing by command as it was done under the period of the law. Instead, the faith-filled Christian is obliged to act on his or her faith, to show prudence towards the ordinance of God and be munificent in all acts of faith. Tithing in this period of grace should be practised with a well balanced and disciplined spiritual mind. The Law is to be noticed as being no longer our tutor but Faith through grace.

The tenth of one's income in this dispensation of great grace is no surprise to send "shock and awe" waves across our faith horizon. The tithe, in fact, is a minimum level to express one's faith, gratitude and generosity to the Lord God in this era of great truth. I honestly believe in truth that, there is much and much more to offer God as a token of our respect and recognition that He alone is our eternal source of supply.

As you keep your covenant or partnership with God, being sincere in all things, including practicing of justice, mercy and faith, to which Scripture refers as **"weightier** matters" (Matt. 23:23), do not neglect this **"weighty** matter" called TITHING, which according to Scripture is "holy" and belongs to the Lord (Lev. 27:30).

FOREWORD

It is a great pleasure for me to write the foreword for this book. I have known Charles Lamptey since 1994. He came to our church looking for a room to start a meeting in Bremen. As a charismatic church within the Fellowship of Pentecostal Churches in Germany (BFP), we gladly offered him a place in our church building. When the meeting grew in size, Charles looked for new premises elsewhere.

Charles loves to write. In this book, he has dared to tackle the topic of "money". In doing so, he reaches into the great treasure of the Bible and explains the divine principle of "giving and receiving." For the reader who is familiar with the giving of the "tithe," his arguments are very understandable. But he also makes it clear how "dangerous" it may be for a child of God not to give the tithe to the Lord.

Anyone who objects that most of the arguments come from the Old Testament must know that, for Jesus and the apostles, this was the only written word of God. The Old Testament makes it clear that "tithing" is not a part of the "law" from which Christ delivered us, for we read as early as Genesis 14:20: *"'And blessed be God Most High, who delivered your enemies into your hand.' Then Abram gave him a tenth of everything."* The written "law" from God was not given until Exodus 24:12. In the New Testament Jesus said, *"Yes, you should tithe, but you shouldn't leave the more important things undone."* (Matthew 23:23, Living Bible).

Now each reader can make the "test," as the word of God suggests in Malachi 3:10: "Bring the whole tithe into the storehouse, that there may be food in my house. Test me in this, says the LORD Almighty, and see if I will not throw open the floodgates of heaven and pour out so much blessing that you will not have room enough for it."

I wish every reader God's blessing and an understanding of the word of God concerning "tithing."

Rev. Werner Gunia,
Former Regional Leader of the Fellowship of Pentecostal Churches (BFP KdöR), Germany

[NB. The *foreword* of this book was written initially for the first edition (in 2005); four years before Pastor Werner Gunia went to be with the LORD. May his righteous soul rest with God in peace!]

INTRODUCTION

There is perhaps no subject that causes greater confusion and contention among the people of God than that of finance. It is one of the topics most spoken of, yet the least understood, declared a beloved servant of God. Church members contend with their leaders, and leaders frustrate their members quite frequently over this delicate subject of finance.

Many great and effective ministries which started very well, growing in size and in the strength of the LORD, experienced their first shockwaves of collapse and "division" when the subject of money was raised and then overemphasized every Sunday from the pulpit.

I once experienced an awful scene in an assembly which split because members asked their leader to account for the specific amount generated by their "generous efforts". I have also heard of a leader who stood before his congregation and boasted about his personal credentials, titles and honour as being much more "valuable" than the amount offered to him each month by the entire congregation, thus belittled their voluntary efforts and generosity.

It is my joy and pleasure to share my heart and understanding concerning this difficult subject of money with you.

God never intended us to be poor. Neither did He say anywhere that "money is evil." Instead, He made Himself very clear through an inspired word found in Paul's first epistle to Timothy, which says,

> *"For the love of money is a root of all kinds of evil......."*
> 1. Timothy 6:10

Thus we see that all the confusion and contention in Christendom concerning tithes and offerings are basically a result of the consuming human craving for money. In his letter to Timothy, the apostle points out the implications of our blind and dangerous passion for material wealth (compare James 4:1-3). No wonder that when Christ entered the temple He chose to sit opposite the treasury (offering bowl). I believe He did so in order to observe and examine the hearts of the people. The Bible says He saw the rich "put in" much, then came a poor widow, who, unlike the rich, "threw in" her two mites.

> *"Jesus sat down opposite the place where the offerings were put and watched the crowd putting their money into the temple treasury. Many rich people threw in large amounts. But a poor widow came and put in [the Greek is literally "threw in"] two copper coins, worth only a fraction of a penny."*
>
> Mark 12:41-42

In the Authorized (King James) Version, the word ***"cast"*** was used to describe the manner in which she gave away her two copper coins, which the Bible says were "all she had to live on" (see Mark 12:44).

It is my firm conviction that this woman, being poor and having no husband to support her, had to struggle within herself for a while before making the final decision to "throw in" all she had. Although she could have been greatly hindered by her poverty and need, her sincere love, mixed with faith and hope in God, was strong enough to neutralize every effort of the devil to quench her desire to give her very best to God.

The Bible says that she "cast" or "threw" her two copper coins into the treasury of the temple — meaning that in the power of faith, hope and love, she vigorously resisted those faithless and discouraging whispers of the devil which could otherwise have prevented her from yielding to God. Desiring to defeat the devil, the poor widow took her last two copper coins, recognized Satan's evil influence on her thoughts, broke through the devilish cycle of deception and "threw" or "cast" the last hope she had in hand (*i.e. her two coins*) into the treasury and thereby obtained that "more excellent hope" which was to be found in the Lord her God and Him alone.

In many other places of Scripture we see the unlimited authority or power of God used in the "casting out" or expulsion of demons, those unclean spirits which can dominate and possess the human soul (and which will not leave voluntarily once they have taken up their residence in the afflicted person). But here we see how the poor widow "cast" (*or, threw energetically*) her last two coins into the treasury. We are not told whether she herself was aware of all the consequences of her action, but she was in fact able to defeat both Satan and the spirit of Mammon by "casting out" her fear of not having the basic necessities of life for the following day.

She "threw" or "cast" into the treasury those coins which the devil could have otherwise used to hinder her from receiving praise and honour from the Lord Jesus Christ. By simply "casting in" (*throwing energetically*) her two mites, she succeeded in "casting out" whole legions of stubborn and wicked spirits, thereby overcoming shame, avarice, ingratitude, hypocrisy, doubt, fear, hopelessness, selfishness and so on, and gaining for herself a "good name," written not in the Guinness Book of Records but, rather, in the Book of Books - the Holy Bible. Hallelujah!

This widow's generous but apparently energetic gesture is a good example for today's believer to follow. When it seems that our money is unwilling to come out of our purses or pockets, we should simply adopt and apply the forceful, energetic method of that poor widow. She did not spend time contemplating on her pressing needs and bills, but simply "threw in" all that she had into the temple treasury, trusting Jehovah-Jireh, the Lord who sees ahead, to provide for her future needs.

The prophet Jeremiah, Moses and the apostle Paul all encourage us to depend on the Lord for our pressing needs since He is the ultimate source of all life. Thus Jeremiah was inspired to say,

> *"For I know the plans I have for you, declares the Lord, plans to prosper you and not to harm you, plans to give you hope and a future."*
>
> Jeremiah 29:11

Using human endeavour to secure your future, without believing God for His supernatural provision and care, may, in the end, prove hopeless and effectually vitiate the result you are trying to achieve.

God once said through Moses,

> *"But remember the Lord your God, for it is He who gives you the ability to produce wealth."*
>
> Deuteronomy 8:18a

Saving or keeping back every cent you receive, and omitting to give tithes and offerings, may never make you rich; for it is the Lord who gives you the power to get wealth. Again, the Bible says,

> *"Not by might nor by power, but by My Spirit, says the Lord Almighty."*
>
> Zechariah 4:6

And the apostle Paul told the early Christians in Corinth:

> *"For you know the grace of our Lord Jesus Christ, that though He was rich, yet for your sakes He became poor, so that you through His poverty might become rich."*
>
> 2. Corinthians 8:9

The poor widow's energetic decision to give to God at such an awkward moment of her life doubtlessly involved a good deal of courage, love, surrender and trust in God. In 1. Timothy 6:10, God simply counsels us to avoid being obsessed, possessed or oppressed by the spirit of Mammon and to equip our minds with His divine understanding and perspective, which in this case means giving obediently to Him the things that belong to Him.

God permits us to possess money and instructs us to be good stewards of it. However, we ourselves are not, to be "possessed" or dominated by it. Unfortunately, it is far easier to love and retain money than it is to give it away for godly purposes. But selfish misappropriation of money is an abomination to God. Even we Christians can develop such an intense love of money that we are not by any means willing to part with it voluntarily. This attitude is what the Bible terms "greed" and can only be overcome by the power, love and sound mind which the Holy Spirit wants to give us as believers.

Today's Christians should be aware that the problems accompanying the subject of money were also common in the days of our Lord Jesus Christ.

The Bible records, for example, the occasion when Jesus went into the temple in Jerusalem and began to overturn the tables of the money changers. His motive in doing this was to restore order, discipline, reverence and prayer to the house of His Father, who delights in faith, love, justice, mercy and obedience much more than in sacrifice (1. Samuel 15:22; Mark 11:15; Matthew 21:12).

The prophet Elisha, King David and the Lord Jesus Himself, tried during their days, to bring about a reformation with regard to the use and understanding of money. In Psalm 15, for example, King David gives us a description of those people who are able to dwell with God on His holy hill. Speaking by the prophetic Spirit, he includes in this description the man *"who lends his money without usury" (Psalm 15:5a).*

Usury means the practise of lending money at a high rate of interest. This is something that God disapproves of, not because it is wrong in itself, but because it is indicative of a wrong and selfish attitude towards one's fellow men. Those to whom the Lord has given a "new heart" and a "new mind" will manifest this even in money-matters!

That is why I believe that in these end-times the members of the household of faith should endeavour to increase their understanding of the biblical doctrine of financial stewardship. This is a very effective way to resist the liar (Satan) and, at the same time, to obviate the danger of greed, dissipation and financial abuse.

Deep in my spirit, I feel there is a widespread need for a more profound understanding of the basic biblical truths concerning money. If correctly applied, these truths could produce much joy and peace among Christians. The result would be an increase in healthy relationships between church members and their leaders, as well as genuine prosperity for the entire body of Christ.

The prophet Elisha once had to rebuke his servant Gehazi for his desire of money. Gehazi had abused God's grace towards the Syrian officer Naaman by secretly asking him for clothing and silver. He was punished for this with a severe plague of leprosy (see 2. Kings 5:20-27). When Elisha perceived the greed of his servant Gehazi, he made the following statement:

> *"Was not my spirit with you when the man got down from his chariot to meet you? **Is this the time to take money?**"*
> 2. Kings 5:26

The answer is clearly and absolutely "no." We are never, I repeat *never*, to take advantage of God's grace in order to enrich ourselves. To partake of the sin of Gehazi for example, by putting psychological pressure on Christians to support "my" ministry is to invite divine retribution and to risk losing that very ministry. There can never be a sufficient reason for taking advantage of the generosity of saved souls merely to fill our own pockets.

Having said this, however, I strongly believe that, in a very different sense, it is indeed now the time for godly people (i.e. the born-again, Spirit-filled Christians) to receive the abundance which God Himself has freely offered us, through the revelation of the suffering of His Son Jesus Christ. I believe this is the time for the saints of Christ to receive the fulness of God's "former and latter rain." It is our time as believers, to receive the accumulated "wealth" of both the gentiles and the wicked, as stated in Scripture (cf. Is. 60:5, 11).

The New Testament makes known to us the mystery of Christ. He was rich beyond comparison in the glory of the Father emptied himself and became poor for our sakes. He was born in a stable and in a manger laid. During His ministry He declared, *"Foxes have holes and birds of the air have nests, but the Son of Man has nowhere to lay His head"* (Luke 9:58). When He needed a coin, a denarius, to prove a point, He had to ask somebody to give Him one (Luke 20:24). In order to pay the temple tax He had to do a miracle and have Peter find the money in the mouth of a fish (Matthew 17:27). When He hung naked on the cross, He was the very image of the most abject poverty.

And yet the Bible makes it clear that *"He became poor, so that you through His poverty might become rich"* (2. Corinthians 8:9). As Christians we are "heirs of God and co-heirs with Christ," called to know the "unsearchable riches of Christ," even the "incomparable riches of His grace, expressed in His kindness to us" (Romans 8:17; Ephesians 3:8; 2:7).

The Lamb of God was slain in order to receive power and wealth and wisdom and strength and honour and glory and praise (Revelation 5:12), and as believers we are now "in Christ," called to share, even in this life, in everything that He has obtained for us. We are no longer to trust in uncertain riches but in the living God, who gives us richly all things to enjoy (1. Timothy 6:17, New King James translation). Wonderful Jesus!

In the Old Testament, the people of Israel received earthly promises. The prophet Isaiah, for example, encouraged the people of Judah in his time with these words:

> *"And you will be called priests of the Lord, you will be named ministers of our God. You will feed on the wealth of the [gentile] nations, and in their riches you will boast."*
>
> Isaiah 61:6

In the New Testament, these earthly promises are filled with a new spiritual meaning. The apostle Peter points out that it is believers in Christ who are now a "royal priesthood" (1. Peter 2:9). Earthly "riches" are "corrupted" (James 5:2 NKJV). For the Bible says, God has chosen those who are poor in the eyes of the world to be rich, not in money, but in faith and to inherit the kingdom He promised to those who love Him (James 2:5).

I strongly believe that it is high time for Christians to enter their inheritance in Christ and "receive exceedingly abundantly above all that they ask or think" (Ephesians 3:20). I believe it is time to receive both peace and joy in His holy presence and, where necessary, a strong financial breakthrough. Satan knows that these things are our due and he is labouring untiringly to confuse our minds with regard to these truths and thus to defeat the end-time church of Christ. But he shall not prevail!

The blessings of the New Covenant, including Christ's riches, are not meant for the mean or avaricious nor for covenant-breakers, but rather for those who are faithful, God-loving and generous according to the revealed will of God. That wonderful verse about Christ becoming *poor* so that we through His poverty might become rich, is given in the context of an apostolic appeal for *generosity*. The apostle Paul, having been greatly blessed and comforted by the generosity of the Philippian Christians, made the following statement in his letter to them:

> *"And my God shall meet all your needs according to His glorious riches in Christ Jesus."*
>
> Philippians 4:19

The apostle Paul only made this statement after he had been totally overwhelmed by the warm, friendly generosity of the Philippian saints. Paul said,

> *"I am amply supplied, now that I have received from Epaphroditus the gifts you sent. They are a fragrant offering, an acceptable sacrifice, pleasing to God."*
>
> Philippians 4:18

As you learn to be generous, faithful and obedient to God's Word, you will not be left unblessed. Rather, God will supply you not merely with some, but with everything you need — according to the power of Christ.

The living Word declares, *"Though it costs all you have, get understanding"* (Proverbs 4:7b). I would therefore encourage you to read on patiently and soberly without doubting the truth of Him who has *"given us everything we need for life and godliness through our knowledge of Him who called us by His own glory and goodness"* (2. Peter 1:3). May the good Lord, to whom alone belong wisdom, knowledge and understanding, enlighten the eyes of your heart and mind by the illuminating power of His Holy Spirit.

CHAPTER 1

THE CONCEPTS OF COVENANT AND GIVING

The Concept of Covenant

A. Definition of a Covenant

The term covenant is one of the most important words found in the Holy Scriptures, occurring some 277 times in the Old Testament and a further 33 times in the New Testament.[1] The Hebrew word for "covenant" is *berith*. This literally means a pledge, a pact, a treaty or an agreement. A covenant may be made between individuals, between a king and his subjects or by God with His chosen people. A covenant can also exist between friends, a man and a woman (in marriage), and between nations.

---

[1] These figures are taken from Robert Young's "Analytical Concordance to the Holy Bible," Guildford and London: Lutterworth Press, 8th ed. Revised, 1939.

It is of prime importance that believers know that they are in a covenant relationship with the Lord, who has chosen them to be the recipients of His grace and mercy towards all who believe in Him. Our God is an awesome God and He has declared that He will keep His covenant "for a thousand generations" (meaning, in today's terminology, "for ever") with all those men and women whom He has "elected" and granted access to His presence by the blood of the Lord Jesus (see Psalm 105:8,9; 1. Peter 1:2; Ephesians 2:18). It is His irrevocable pledge that He will be God to us for ever as He was to Abraham.

B. Purposes of a Covenant

Every covenant God makes with man involves three major aspects:

1. The *promise* of the covenant.
2. The *condition* of the covenant.
3. The *sign* of the covenant.

* God *promises* always to bless, save, heal, restore, deliver and exalt those whom He chooses to make His covenant partners. And as God, **who cannot lie** (cf. Numbers 23:19; Titus 1:2), is always faithful to His word. **His promises never fail**. Even when sinful men fail to obey and to be constantly faithful, God remains true to Himself: *"If we are faithless, He will remain faithful, for He cannot disown Himself"* (2. Timothy 2:13-NIV).

* By His *condition,* God requires faithfulness and covenant loyalty from those who are privileged to be in a covenant relationship with Him. *"If we disown Him, He will also disown us" (2. Timothy 2:12).* That was made very clear in the context of the Old Testament (which also could be referred to as the "Old Covenant"), in which God announced severe penalties for both disloyalty and disobedience. God did not hesitate to discipline the wayward children of Israel, a common example of which we find in Deuteronomy 28:15-68 (compare 2. Kings 17:7-23). Therefore, if even in the Old Testament era (when Christ had not yet finally redeemed His people), God stated the necessity for punishing His people (Isaiah 28:21), how much more shall He tolerate the New Testament believers who have been "justified freely by His grace through the redemption that came by Christ Jesus" (Romans 3:24). As the redeemed of the Lord we have "peace with God through our Lord Jesus Christ, through whom we have gained access into this grace in which we now stand" (Romans 5:1-2), for which reason *"there is now no condemnation to those who are in Christ Jesus" (Romans 8:1).* "For I am convinced," writes the apostle Paul, "that neither death nor life, neither angels nor demons, neither the present nor the future, nor any powers, neither height nor depth, nor anything else in all creation, will be able to separate us from the love of God that is in Christ Jesus our Lord" (Romans 8:38-39).

It is the essence of God to be full of love and compassion to all, especially to His children. God's grace and faithfulness are two of His most outstanding attributes, and it was these attributes that prompted Him to promise a new land to the Israelites (compare Exodus 12:25 3:7-8) and to fulfil that promise in spite of all their disobedience. It was also, of course, the grace and faithfulness of God that led Him to fulfil all the promises made to His friend Abraham by sending Jesus Christ to be our Redeemer and Baptizer in the Holy Spirit (Galatians 3:14).

Because God is faithful, He also promises to be with the upright in all their troubles (Psalm 91:15) and to deliver them out of them (Psalm 34:19). No matter how great our afflictions may be, no matter what persecutions we may suffer, if we are in Christ Jesus, then the Lord will be with us and ruling over every situation for our good.

Let us turn to aspect number two, the *condition* of the covenant. If we as Christians are God's covenant partners, we may well be asking on what conditions we remain in fellowship with Him. Under the old covenant, the condition was undoubtedly *obedience.* It was part of the very fabric of God's covenant dealings with Israel that obedience to the law brought God's blessing with it, which usually meant victory over enemies and external prosperity. Disobedience, on the other hand, was to bring down God's curse on His covenant people.[2] The problem was, of course, that not even the people of Israel, with all

---

[2] This is stated especially clearly in Deuteronomy chapter 28.

their covenant privileges, could ever really obey God's law. As the apostle Paul shows so clearly in the letter to the Romans, the law itself was "holy, righteous and good," (Romans 7:12) but the power of indwelling sin in natural man was so great that it perverted even God's holy law and turned it into an instrument of sin and death (Romans 7:10 ff.). The historical and prophetic books of the Old Testament with their record of the sad failings of God's people offer a tragic commentary on this truth. But at the same time, they ever and again offer glimpses of the wonderful way in which God intended to solve this problem. The prophet Jeremiah, for example, whose writings are generally characterized by gloom and judgement, comes up at one point with a wonderful promise:

> *"The time is coming," declares the Lord, "when I will make a new covenant with the house of Israel and the house of Judah. It will not be like the covenant I made with their forefathers when I took them by the hand to lead them out of Egypt, because they broke my covenant, though I was a husband to them," declares the Lord. "This is the covenant that I will make with the house of Israel after that time," declares the Lord.* ***"I will put my law in their minds and write it on their hearts"***
>
> Jeremiah 31:13-33

The prophet Ezekiel took this up and added a further insight: *"I will give you a new heart and put a new spirit in you; I will remove from you your heart of stone and give you a heart of flesh. And I will put my Spirit in you and move you to follow my decrees and be careful to keep my laws" (Ezekiel 36:26 ff.).*

When Jesus came, He taught people to expect a "new birth" (John 3:3 and cf. 1. Peter 1:3) that would be accompanied by an outpouring of the Holy Spirit (compare Luke 3:16 with John 7:38 ff.). He then went voluntarily to the Cross as our substitute and sin-offering. Through His death He bore for us the "curse" of the law, that is, the curse that was due to us because of our disobedience, thus making us "righteous" before God and earning for us the right to be God's children and as such "no longer under the law, but under grace" (Galatians 3:13; Romans 3:24; 5:1; John 1:12; Romans 8:15 ff.; 6:14). Because we are "united with Christ in His death," we have entered a new spiritual realm in which the Holy Spirit gives us His life and His power to live the kind of life that God always wanted His people to live. The apostle Paul sums it all up in those tremendous words:

> *"Therefore, there is now no condemnation for those who are in Christ Jesus, because through Christ Jesus the law [principle] of the Spirit of life set me free from the [old covenant] law of sin and death. For what the law was powerless to do in that it was weakened*

> *by the sinful nature, God did by sending His own Son in the likeness of sinful man to be a sin-offering. And so He condemned sin in sinful man in order that the righteous requirements of the law might be fully met in us, who do not live according to the sinful nature but according to the Spirit."*
>
> Romans 8:1-4

The Lord Jesus has actually done what the prophets foretold. Through Him God has created a new covenant people who live for Him by the power of the Holy Spirit. Under the old covenant, fellowship with God was only possible through obedience and sacrifice. Jesus Christ accomplished our salvation by offering His Father a life of perfect sinless obedience and then bringing the supreme sacrifice of His own life as a sin-offering for all who would believe in Him. Under the new covenant, fellowship with God is possible because of His obedience and His sacrifice. Of course Christians want to obey this wonderful Saviour, but their motivation is no longer that of fear — fear of the curse, fear of the wrath and punishment of God. Their motivation is the motivation of love.

* ***The sign of the covenant***: after sharing with Abraham the conditions for all His covenant promises, God then gave him the sign (or seal) of the covenant (Genesis 17:10 ff.). Circumcision marked the entrance of all that were born to Abraham into the covenant. It was the sign of the Abrahamic covenant.

As Spirit-filled, New Testament Christians, we — unlike the patriarchs — live under a better covenant, made not by *the blood of bulls* and *goats* but by **the blood of the precious Lamb of God – Jesus Christ of Nazareth**. The Scriptures declare that His blood "speaks better things" even than the blood of righteous Abel (Hebrews 12:24).

The blood of Jesus graciously speaks of mercy and pardon whenever we fall short of the Lord's glory and plead with him for forgiveness. If we truly repent, we are reconciled to God the Father by the power of the blood and restored to unbroken fellowship with Him. Because God was perfectly aware of our human frailties even before he made us, He provided for all our weaknesses through the Holy Spirit, who was to be given us as a fruit of our covenant relationship with him (compare Romans 8:26 with Galatians 3:14; 5:16). He has fully paid the price for our sins. That is why He was able to declare through one of the Old Covenant prophets:

> *"Come now, let us reason together," says the Lord. "Though your sins are like scarlet, they shall be as white as snow; though they are red as crimson, they shall be like wool. If you are willing and obedient, you will eat the best of the land; but if you resist and rebel, you will be*

devoured by the sword." For the mouth of the Lord has spoken.

Isaiah 1:18 ff.

Now read this again, not just with your eyes, but also with your understanding. The price of all your mistakes and of your every misdeed has been paid for fully by means of the sacrificial death of our Lord and Saviour Jesus Christ on the Cross of Calvary.

Hence, as a loyal covenant-partner, all you need to do if you fall into sin, is to call out for His mercy in genuine repentance and He will hear you. Never quit the race of faith because *"winners do not quit,"* and remember that, *"quitters cannot win"*. Do not seek to break off your covenant relationship with the Lord, because by doing that you would be cutting yourself off from the only source of grace, life and forgiveness. But if only you call on him, there is always hope, and you will be enabled to rise up from where you have fallen.

The enemy always desires to keep you down when you fail and fall in your covenant walk with God, but God himself has promised never to surrender you to the desire of your foes (Psalm 41:2). The enemy of your soul seeks for an opportunity to rejoice over you the moment you fall. But even when you are in the "pit" or the "mire of despond," you should never keep your mouth shut, which would be tantamount to admitting defeat; instead, you should declare in the hearing of all your adversaries:

> *"Do not gloat over me, my enemy. Though I have fallen, I will rise. Though I sit in darkness, the LORD will be my light."*
>
> Micah 7:8

Shake yourself, make this faith-filled declaration and refuse to remain in your fallen position. Rather, rise up in the name of the Lord Jesus Christ and press on!

The journey that the children of the covenant have to make is indeed very long, the way is sometimes high and sometimes very deep. Your faith will be tried many times, your love for God will be tested as by fire, but by this even your will will be brought into submission to Him who owns everything you have and are. Never forget these truths:

> **"You were cut for the conflict;
> you were built for the battle;
> you were prepared for the war;
> you are a prevailer and not a wailer;
> you are a champion over thousands and
> ten thousands;
> you are a winner in all wars."**

No matter whether you fail, faint or fall, God's promises are ever sure; He will strengthen you, He will quicken you and raise you up before the enemy can gain control over you.

Never listen to the lies Satan whispers to you. Do not permit him to gain the advantage over you and to deprive you of future blessings. Do not allow him to use your past mistakes to rob you of your present glory and honour. For you are what God says you are and not what the enemy says or thinks you are. Of course, you ought not to sin wilfully against the Lord, yet you are assured by the infallible Word of God that you will be raised upon your feet seven times if necessary (Proverbs 24:16) in order to prove to God's enemies that there is none good apart from the Lord, the only Saviour of mankind. Hallelujah!

As a child of God you are a partaker of a covenant which is established on better promises, is sealed with a better sign and granted on better conditions than anything the Old Testament saints were privileged to know. Under the Abrahamic covenant Abraham himself and the patriarchs who came after him were designated "servants," but under the New Covenant believers in Christ, having been reconciled to God, are designated "sons," and if sons, then heirs and joint heirs with Christ before the throne of God (Romans 8:16 ff.).

> *"He came to that which was his own, but his own did not receive Him. Yet to all who received Him, to those who believed in his name, he gave the right to become children of God."*
>
> John 1:11 ff.

Just as circumcision was the covenant sign given to every child born of Abraham, even so our faith is the outward, visible sign that we have been "born from above" into the New Covenant Kingdom of God by the power of the precious, redeeming blood of the Lord Jesus Christ. Our sins are forgiven, and we are the children of God. Praise His Name!

The Concept of Giving

Both *giving* and *receiving* are constituent aspects of our **covenant** (*in Heb.- "berith"*) with God. A covenant by which we are made to become God's children through Christ Jesus our Lord.

Now under the *concept of giving,* we can differentiate *three types* of "giving":

1.) **GOD** *giving* to man;
2.) **MAN** *giving* to God;
3.) **MAN** *giving* to man.

God giving to Man

In Genesis 1:1 we read, *"In the beginning God created ..."* This is an indication that there was never any other God, not even before the world existed. The Bible declares that "before Him there was no other god neither shall there be any after Him" (Isaiah 43:10-11). The literal meaning of God's name "Jehovah Elohim" is a revelation of His self-existing nature. He is the God that *was* before anything else could be, He is the One who creates and sustains all things, and He will be revealed to all humanity in time to come.

Since there was neither any human being nor any other superhuman being around before the creation, the Scripture ascribes the glory of creation and the full ownership of the entire universe to God. It was He who created all things. The Bible literally states, "All things were created by Him" (Colossians 1:16). God is the source of life for all creation. And God freely gave to His creation, especially to man, all that He — God — stood for, a free gift of Himself to humanity, serving as a perfect example for all men to follow.

No man could boast of having first given anything to Him that needed to be paid back. No! Instead, God in His eternal self-existent state first gave all things to man: breath for life, water and food for strength, the sun and the moon for light, and so on.

The Bible says,

> "For God [the Creator] so loved the world that He gave [He didn't take, but rather first gave] His one and only Son, that whoever believes in him shall not perish but have eternal life."
>
> John 3:16

The good God goes on giving and forgiving, whereas the evil one, Satan, seeks to take away what is given to us by our good God.

God has never stopped giving good things to men. The Scripture says,

> *"He who did not spare His own Son, but gave Him up for us all — how will He not also, along with Him, graciously give us all things?"*
> Romans 8:32

Behind every good or perfect gift is love; therefore it is by the great love with which He loves us that He freely gives us all things for our good. We would be wise to understand that God is the absolute source of life, blessing and true peace for His entire creation. We read for instance in Genesis 2:7 that it was God who first breathed life into the created being called man. Study these further examples:

(1) After the world sinned and fell short of the glory of God (Romans 3:23), God gave His Son Jesus Christ to die on the Cross to redeem us from our sins (John 3:16).

(2) When Abraham and Sarah were old and had no child, God gave them Isaac to fulfil the promise He had previously made to Abraham (Genesis 21:2).

(3) When the children of Israel were famishing in the wilderness and there was no bread for them to

eat, God gave them fresh manna each morning for breakfast (Deuteronomy 8:16).

(4) When the Israelites complained bitterly that they had no meat to eat, God once more, performed a miracle and gave them meat in the form of quails to eat until they were sick of it (Numbers 11:31).

(5) When the Israelites came face to face with the Red Sea and there was no boat to cross them over to the other side, God incredibly provided them a way of escape through the sea.

He gave them water to quench their thirst and protection throughout their journey in the wilderness — a pillar of cloud by day and of fire by night.

God has not changed. He is still the same yesterday, today and forever (Hebrews 13:8). Hallelujah! God will also act on your behalf if you can only believe.

Man giving to God

> *"Be imitators of God, therefore, as dearly loved children and live a life of love, just as Christ loved us and gave Himself up for us as a fragrant offering and sacrifice to God."*
>
> Ephesians 5:1 ff.

Having been instructed by God's personal example of giving, man began to walk in the Lord's footsteps. Thus it was that righteous Abel, by offering a better sacrifice than his elder brother Cain, honoured the Lord with his property and was himself honoured by God, who spoke well of his offerings (Genesis 4:4; Hebrews 11:4).

Abraham, too, having tasted the generosity of God in the birth of Isaac, learnt to reciprocate God's love and was even prepared to sacrifice his one and only son, the joy and delight of his old age (Genesis 22:9 ff.).

After many years of tears, Hannah also, having received the child Samuel from the Lord in answer to prayer, devoted him to the Lord's service (1. Samuel 1:27 ff.).

Receiving from God is a tremendous blessing, but giving back to Him is an act of *l*ove, *o*bedience and *w*orship: ***low*** - a way of ***low***ering or humbling yourself before the Lord and thereby allowing Him to exalt you.

Giving back to God things that belong to Him is one of the most perfect ways of expressing our faith in the Lord. God must be honoured because He is the Father of all creation and must be feared because He is the Master of the whole universe.

> *"'A son honours his father, and a servant his master. If I am a father, where is the honour due to me? If I am a master, where is the respect due to me?' says the Lord Almighty. 'It is you, O priests, who show contempt for my name. But you ask, "How have we shown contempt for your name?"'"*
>
> Malachi 1:6

People have shown great contempt for the name of the Lord in the areas of giving and receiving. God has given so much to humanity and has received but little or nothing at all in return. Solomon, that wise king of Israel, gave us more than a hint as to how we should honour the Lord when he wrote,

> *"Honour the Lord with your wealth, with the firstfruits of all your crops; then your barns will be filled to overflowing, and your vats will brim over with new wine."*
>
> Proverbs 3:9 ff.

You need only mustard-seed faith (not mega-faith) to honour the Lord with the wealth He has given you.

And if you happen to think that what you have in hand is too little to meet even your own needs, then you should be aware that if you sow it in faith, you will reap a bountiful harvest (2. Corinthians 9:6-11).

Man giving to Man

Giving from one man to another is an honourable and acceptable practise before the Lord. When one Christian gives to another, this is a practical expression of the love of God. Furthermore, an exchange of gifts between men enhances their mutual relationship and strengthens their human bonds. It inspires love, peace and spiritual rapport between giver and receiver and thereby promotes unity and stability among those who practise it.

In exile on the island of Patmos, the apostle John had the following message for his brothers and sisters in Christ:

> *"If anyone says, 'I love God', yet hates his brother, he is a liar."*
>
> 1. John 4:20

We do not show our love for God with mere empty words, but by works of faith, performed on the basis of our spiritual understanding. Until the eye of your understanding is enlightened to know the hope with which He has called you (Ephesians 1:18), you may never realize how important it is to be prepared to give to your fellow-man.

In this glorious kingdom of God we are called to be "one another's keeper." This means that we are not supposed constantly to "mind our own business." God is, indeed, capable of doing all things directly, but He sees fit to help and bless us by inspiring sincere, loving, mutual relationships between man and man through the effective work of His Holy Spirit.

God loves mankind because He created us. We are His, and He seeks daily to nurture, nourish and assist us in all our areas of need. God's normal way of doing this is not by a supernatural display of His omnipotence. Rather, God delights in using human beings as His extended arm to minister aid to other human beings. Hence, the practise of helping, caring and giving to others is a wonderful expression of the love of God in action.

Giving to our fellow men or receiving from them, is a way of imitating God's example of generosity. When we give gifts to a fellow man on the basis of sincere love, it is recognized and esteemed by God as gift offered to Him. This is why the Scripture declares that, "If anyone says 'I love God,' yet hates his brother, he is a liar." This simply means that you cannot boldly declare with mere words nor even with gifts that you love God if your affection towards your brother or sister, whom you daily see suffering, weeping or at the point of death, is lacking.

No teaching or activity contrary to the statement of love in 1. John 4:20 will ever yield spiritual fruit. If we desire God's blessing for our life and work, we must realize that He expects us to be helpful towards our fellow human beings and, particularly, towards those who "belong to the family of believers" (Galatians 6:10). The Bible encourages us to do good to our fellow men just as if we were doing it directly to the Lord Himself.

Elijah the prophet once received the following word from the Lord:

> *"Go at once to Zarephath, of Sidon and stay there. I have commanded a widow in that place to provide you with food."*
> 1. Kings 17:9

Although this widow was very poor and had nothing but a handful of flour in a bin and a little oil in a jar, she was used by God to provide for His servant Elijah. Elijah was a prophet of God but the widow thought that she was dealing with a normal human being. In fact, when they first met, she saw nothing but a mere man who was hungry and looking for food to eat. And, indeed, she could have refused Elijah's request, just as many other people in those days did, who deliberately ignored and despised the Lord's commandment. But she did not.

Instead, regardless of her poverty and great need, she responded positively to the request of the man of God and as a result of her obedience, reaped a miraculous blessing from the Lord. This is a marvellous example of what can happen when we are prepared to give to one another.

In 2. Kings 4:8, the Bible tells us about a well-to-do woman from Shunem who, seeing Elisha pass by, persuaded him to stay for a meal and also prepared a place of rest for him on the roof of her house. Her love and generosity towards this servant of God opened a door of blessing on her life and family; until this time she had been barren, but now she was delivered and made fruitful by the power of the God of Elisha. This again was, in the sovereignty of God, the fruit of an exchange of gifts between fellow human beings. Loving and giving to one's fellow man is, in the Lord's eyes, equivalent to loving and serving Him.

Helping our fellow human beings, especially if they are God's children or, indeed, His ministers, is recognized by the Lord as being done for Him and not just as something we do for other people.

God strongly backs up every good work we do to secure, help, protect or deliver fellow human beings from pain or death. The blessing of the One who bled on Calvary's hill always follows every good work done by a man to his neighbour.

For this reason, anyone who claims to love God must also make plain that he loves man. Jesus said the second commandment is exactly like the first:

> *"Love the Lord your God with all your heart and with all your soul and with all your mind and with all your strength.." [This is the first commandment.] "The second is this: 'Love your neighbour as yourself'. There is no commandment greater than these."*
>
> Mark 12:30 ff.

In another place the Scripture says,

> *"Do not say to your neighbour, 'Come back later; I'll give it tomorrow' — when you now have it with you."*
>
> Proverbs 3:28

In the Gospel of Luke we read,

> *"Give, and it will be given to you. A good measure, pressed down, shaken together and running over, will be poured into your lap. For with the measure you use, it will be measured to you."*
>
> Luke 6:38

The Scripture goes on to say that,

> *"Anyone who receives instruction in the word must share all good things with his instructor. Do not be deceived: God cannot be mocked. A man reaps what he sows. [...] Let us not become weary in*

doing good, for at the proper time we will reap a harvest if we do not give up. Therefore, as we have opportunity, let us do good to all people, especially to those who belong to the family of believers."
Galatians 6:6-7,9-10

Reciprocal giving and receiving is one of the basic Christian privileges and duties. Those who practise it will never be put to shame. Giving and receiving from each other according to the will of the Lord is a way of enhancing our mutual peace, love and joy in the Lord. Do not stop caring for each other. Continue to be each other's keeper. God desires you to maintain the unity of the Spirit through unstinting love of the brethren.

Satan Wants to Hinder You

Satan is a liar and has been the father of lies from the beginning. He devises all manner of deception and thinks up fraudulent, wicked, evil schemes. Not content with that, he goes on to create a strong resistance against any progress among God's people. He resists every thought of faith, love and hope in order to hamper the development of the believer's spiritual life. His very name, Satan, depicts his nature – a "resister."

God earnestly exhorts us to bring "the whole tithe" into the storehouse that there may be food in His house,

(Malachi 3:10) but Satan (the resister) and his ministers (the demons) never permit you to bring your complete tithes into the church with ease. They will do everything in their power to discourage and frustrate your mind by directing it towards your own pressing needs, thus causing you to go against what the God of the covenant has expressed as His sovereign will for your life. Satan and his agents will put pressure on your soul to make you feel helpless and hopeless, and their object in doing so is to make you give up every ray of hope or confidence the Lord would offer. Satan's goal is to trap you and force you to succumb to his diabolical deceptions. One of these is to focus your gaze on your present pressing needs and thereby cause you to abandon your decision to be obedient to the Lord.

The very moment he succeeds in influencing you to magnify your needs above your faith in God's word, you fail to honour God faithfully in the realm of giving.

Remember what is said concerning the devil in John 8:44 and 10:10. He is a thief and a liar from the beginning and all he can get you to do is to make you to be like him: a thief and a liar; but you must steadfastly refuse and resist him in the name of the Lord Jesus Christ.

Join me now in faith to pray this prayer:

"I am strong in the Lord and in the power of His might.

As a prince, I have power with God and with men and have prevailed.

No weapon formed against me shall prosper, and I condemn any tongue which rises against me.

For I wrestle not against flesh and blood but against Satan and his hosts of wickedness.

My victory over Satan is not obtained by might nor by power but by the "burden-removing," "yoke-destroying" power of the Holy Spirit.

For the Lord is my strength, my shield and my exceeding great reward.

In Him I live, in Him I move and in Him I have my being.

Now with the armour of God, I resist the resister and destroy the destroyer in the mighty Name of Jesus Christ.

I have raised my hand to the Lord even to God Most High, the Possessor of heaven and earth, who gives me the power to acquire wealth and strikes the belly of my enemies to vomit up my stolen treasures.

In the Name of the Lord Jesus Christ I free myself from the wicked influence of the devil and proceed forth to be a cheerful giver even from this time forth and for ever more. Amen."

In Titus 1:2, the Bible reveals that God cannot lie. Therefore, when He declares that what you give will be given back to you, and that a good measure, pressed down, shaken together and running over will be poured into your lap, then He means what He says.

God's Word fully assures us that the labour of His righteous servants will never be in vain.

Therefore, make yourself available to God. Ask Him to teach and bless you as you humbly learn to be a generous giver both to God and to your fellow man.

CHAPTER 2

TITHES AND TAXES

During His ministry, the Lord Jesus Christ was once confronted by the Pharisees concerning tax-paying. They cunningly put Him to test in order to find fault with His teachings and asked Him, "Tell us then, what is Your opinion? Is it right to pay taxes to Caesar or not?" But the Lord Jesus, perceiving their wicked intention, responded, "You hypocrites, why are you trying to trap me? Show me the coin used for paying the tax." And when they had brought him a denarius (Jesus obviously did not have one Himself), he asked, "Whose portrait is this? And whose inscription?" And the Bible tells us that the Pharisees correctly answered, "Caesar's". Then Jesus said to them,

> *"Give to Caesar what is Caesar's, and to God what is God's."*
>   See Matthew 22:15-22

With this wise answer, the Lord Jesus disrupted their evil schemes and thereby drew a clear line between the things that belong lawfully to Caesar and those things that also belong to God: We can summarize what He wanted to say under the headings: *"Taxes to Caesar"* and *"Tithes to God."*

Dealing with Caesar's Taxes

What is Tax?

A **tax** is a compulsory payment levied by a government on income, property etc. in order to raise revenue.

My simplest definition for **TAX** is - Caesar's "**T**ree - **AX**e". In Matthew's Gospel we read the following words declared by John the Baptist,-

> *"The **axe** is already at the root of the **trees**, and every tree that does not produce good fruit will be cut down and thrown into the fire."*
>
> Matthew 3:10

Now, John the Baptist was certainly not speaking about Caesar and his kingdom, but his statement could well be applied to Caesar's motives and intentions: Caesar's "tree-axe" is already at the root of his citizens' income; and any citizen living in *"Caesarland"* who refuses to pay the tax is to expect a certain harsh and severe punishment. The miscreant may be *"cut down"* (i.e., *sent to prison*) for the act of apparent disobedience. This further means, any citizen of Caesar's kingdom who refuses to pay his or her taxes is liable to be confronted and be dealt with by Caesar's law enforcement officers.

Caesar, (as the supreme ruler) expects every citizen of his country to be *loyal* in all matters concerning taxation. In his view, reluctance to pay the state tax is considered unpatriotic. He equates the act to rebellion against national *authority* and therefore should be mete out with punishment.Now with the power invested in his authority, Caesar could use his **T**ree-A**X**e to *cut down* any person in his kingdom who does not bear fruit to raise the revenue needed by the national government.

In countries like Germany and other European nations, taxes on income are in many cases automatically deducted from a person's wages before he or she receives them. The government and the inland revenue office, however, care less about the employee's (or the tax payer's) *private* difficulties. They do not ask if the employee has sufficient money to live on or not, and they only take account of a person's marital status and debts up to a certain sum. The taxpayer's personal situation or comfort is just not something they are interested in. They are rather interested in implementing the law which lays down that taxes are to be automatically deducted from wages in order to raise revenue for the state. There can be no argument about this. Taxes lawfully belong to

"Caesar", that is, to the ruling authority that governs a nation or a country.

Jesus wisely counselled His disciples to give to Caesar everything that belongs to him. Jesus did not call for a revolution against Rome, despite the fact that the Romans had conquered the Jews and were also their oppressors. I am convinced that He knew the damage which "blind disobedience" could bring to the church if she refuses to obey Caesar's law. Jesus was fully aware that Caesar did not only stretch out one hand to receive taxes, but also he was ready to act violently with his *tree-axe* to afflict anyone who stood against his desire.

The Spirit-filled Christian is also called upon to bear with his government wherever possible, since law and order must be maintained to avoid any anarchy. Even when a state government denies people the liberty to worship and obey God freely, as the Roman government was to do in later years, Christians are called upon to "submit themselves to the governing authorities" (Romans 13:1). There is only one exception to this rule: where laws are made which would force Christians to disobey their Lord, believers must join with Peter and the other apostles in saying, "We must obey God rather than men!" (Acts 5:29).

We find out that paying taxes was deemed right by the Lord Himself as He encouraged His followers to give to Caesar that which he had the right to demand. In today's terms, Christians, like all citizens of all nations are to offer taxes to their ruling local government who are elected by the people to care for the land or the country. Blind disobedience towards instituted rule of law concerning secular matters which are not offensive to the Word of Truth could lead to absolute anarchy in any system or in any country.

Let's take a quick look at the passage from Romans chapter 13:

> *"Everyone must submit himself to the governing authorities, for there is no authority except that which God has established. The authorities that exist have been established by God. Consequently, he who rebels against the authority is rebelling against what God has instituted, and those who do so will bring judgment on themselves. For rulers hold no terror for those who do right, but for those who do wrong. [...] For he is God's servant to do you good. But if you do wrong, be afraid; for he does not bear the sword for nothing. He is God's servant, an agent of wrath to bring punishment on the wrongdoer. [...] Give everyone what you owe him: If you owe taxes, pay taxes; if revenue, then revenue; if respect, then respect; if honour, then honour."*
>
> Romans 13:1-4,7

In his teaching on submission to rulers and authorities, Paul remained steadfast. Towards the end of his life, he wrote the following words to his fellow-worker Titus, words which surely apply today just as much as they did nearly 2000 years ago:

> *"Remind the people to be subject to rulers and authorities, to be obedient, to be ready to do whatever is good, to slander no-one, to be peaceable and considerate, and to show true humility to all men. [...] This is a trustworthy saying. And I want you to stress these things, so that those who have trusted in God may be careful to devote themselves to doing what is good. These things are excellent and profitable for everyone."*
>
> Titus 3:1-2,8

Dealing with God's Holy Tithe

Unlike taxes, **tithes** belong to God. When this is recognized and well understood, we would bring all the tithe to the prescribed place, which is the house of God. Just as the tax is given to "Caesar" or our local government, the tithe is brought to the treasure of the church of Christ. Hence, taxes belong to Caesar (to our local government); and tithes belong to God. Therefore also Jesus said we should give to Caesar what belongs to Caesar and to God that which belongs to Him.

What is Tithe?

A tithe is the tenth of one's income or produce paid or given to God. It is one of God's divine sources of revenue, raised to enhance the progress and expansion of His Church and kingdom on earth. Originally (i.e., under the old covenant,) tithes were basically used to *care for*; (i) the priests in God's house, (ii) the temple/tabernacle, and (iii) for strangers and the fatherless. However, the *priests* themselves also gave back to the Lord *a tenth* of all the tithe they received from the people. They were to be examples to the entire congregation of Israel.

Mathematical Calculation

So, for instance, if John Smith receives a monthly net income of € 1,500, and supposing John Smith is to be a faithful Christian who is obedient in the matter of giving the tithe, he would desire to give one tenth of his income as a tithe to the storehouse of God (that is, to the church to which he belongs), i.e. $1/10 \times 1{,}500 = €\ 150$. Since one tenth of € 1,500 is € 150, he would willingly offer this amount to God. He would recognize that this is God's portion, to be used for the blessing and furtherance of the work of Christ in his locality and in missionary work. And of course, he would give voluntarily, with a grateful heart, rejoicing in what the Lord had done for him and would continue to do through him and through his financial contribution to the work of the gospel.

Under the new covenant, there is no legal requirement to give (compare Acts 5:4 with 2. Corinthians 9:7). But reluctance to give is a sign that a Christian has lost sight of the debt he owes to his Lord and Saviour, who not only gave everything up for him but also went voluntarily to that bitter death on the cross in order to save him from eternal damnation.

Let me use an acronym: **T**ithing **I**s **T**he **H**oly **E**ntry or key to true partnership with God. In God's promise to Israel by Malachi we are made to understand that, tithing is the true key which "opens the floodgates of heaven," for God to pour out so much blessing that one cannot have room enough to contain it (cf. Malachi 3:10). If you give or bring the tithe to the storehouse of God, God promises (i) to "prevent pests from devouring your crops;" (ii) "that your vine shall not fail to bear fruit in your fields (iii) and that you shall be called blessed among all the nations of the world (Malachi 3:11-12). God is not pressing upon us some unpleasant duty or tedious task to perform rather, he offers us a gracious means to attain His blessings. Beloved, tithing to God leads to blessing!

CHAPTER 3

THE INSTITUTION OF TITHING

In Leviticus, we find the answer to the question, Who instituted tithing?

> *"A tithe of everything from the land [...] belongs to the Lord; it is holy to the Lord."*
> Leviticus 27:30

From the scripture above, we understand that tithing was instituted by God and thus He considers it to be holy. Hence, what God considers as holy must also be treated as holy. Therefore, handling the issue of tithing with contempt or disregard, would involve us in sacrilege, which would doubtless bring dire consequences.

One of the reasons why many church members are poor and not prosperous is that they have, out of ignorance, profaned God's holy institution of tithing. According to Malachi 3:9, God does not tolerate this form of ignorance: "You are under a curse [...], because you are robbing Me". The outworkings of this curse are the misery and wretchedness which we see in many so-called Christian homes today.

Entire nations and lands have become impoverished simply because of their ignorance about giving to God the things that belong to Him – "a tithe of everything from the land" (Leviticus 27:30).

Unless people recognize tithing as an important issue and as a divine ordinance that should be complied with, the shackles of poverty will not be broken off their necks and feet. It takes God and His yoke-breaking, burden-removing power to overcome the deceiver, whose aim is ever to manoeuvre us from honour into dishonour, from grace to disgrace, from praise to pain. For the Scripture reveals that, "It is not by strength that one prevails," (cf. 1. Samuel 2:9); and we know from the written word of God that, "it is not by might nor by power but by My Spirit, says the Lord Almighty" (Zechariah 4:6).

The Commencement of Tithe Paying

When Did It Start?

Tithing began from the time God started blessing mankind — right from the time when man started harvesting what he had planted, and when he started receiving wages or income from his labour.

We find a very early example at the time of the patriarch Abraham who, according to the clear statements of both the Old and the New Testaments, met Melchizedek (the king of Salem) after his return from battle and gave him one-tenth of all he had gained (Genesis 14:18 ff.). And having received Abraham's tithe, Melchizedek blessed him. This is surely a type or shadow of things to come: when we as Christians bring the tithe to Jesus, our great High Priest, He too, will bless us!

Jacob, Abraham's grandson, made a vow at Bethel to give God one tenth of all that he would gain if God would only protect him and bring him back safely to his father's house (Genesis 28:20 ff.). And the God who cannot lie (but keeps covenant to a thousand generations) went beyond mere protection and delivered him completely from the vengeful hand of his brother Esau. Jacob was richly blessed by the ever-faithful God in spite of his "if-clause."

As New Covenant people, we have a better understanding of tithing than Jacob, so it would be quite absurd to imitate him by adopting his conditional clause. It is ours today to trust and obey. But we may indeed learn from Jacob that if we trust and obey, we can expect God to watch over us and protect us from our enemies!

When Do We Begin to Tithe?

As a principle, every Christian is called to bring a tenth of his or her income into God's "storehouse", the local church or assembly. Let me be quite specific about this. You are called to tithe:

(i) from the very day you become a member of the body of Christ, i.e. when you accept Jesus as your personal Lord and Saviour and agreed with Him in your heart to become His servant;

(ii) from the moment when you start receiving wages or salary;

(iii) whenever God shows you kindness, protects you and provides for you — even when you are not earning wages.

It is a worthy thing in the Kingdom of God that we offer thanks to Him for the blessings received. One very fitting way of doing this is by giving the tithe. It is only if you have not been blessed at all and have absolutely no source of income and nothing to give that you would have an adequate reason for not tithing. God does not expect us to give what He has not first given us. But when He has given richly, is it too much to ask that we return a meagre ten percent to show our gratitude?

Please do not misunderstand me at this point. It is not my intention to lay the law down and bring you into bondage. No, I want to see Christians everywhere enjoying "the glorious *freedom* of the children of God" (Romans 8:21). Freedom from social, political, economical and financial bondages. But notice that liberty from financial difficulty is not a licence for one to rob God of His rights and dues. It is only when we yield to the Spirit and "put to death the misdeeds of the body" (Romans 8:13) that we will enjoy the fulness and blessing of our new life in Christ. If the doctrine of tithing is new to you and you find it a challenge, then all I can say is, try it and see! God has promised to protect, bless and greatly increase those men and women who "live by faith," and living by faith means trusting Him to ensure that I will not be at a disadvantage for obeying His Word!

CHAPTER 4

WHY TITHING WAS INSTITUTED BY GOD

There are three important reasons why God has instituted tithing:

(1) We tithe so that there may be "food" in God's house. Food is a basic resource needed by every human being in order to survive. In this, the ministers of God's church are no exception. In order for them to be able to fulfil their ministry and "feed" the flock of God properly, they themselves need sustenance. There may be exceptions, as in the case of the apostle Paul (see Acts 18:3; 20:33; 1. Corinthians 9:15), but in the normal run of things God expects the members of Christian churches to provide for their ministers by means of tithes and offerings, so that these men or women may devote themselves fully to the ministry to which they have been called. This

is the simplest and most basic reason why God has instituted tithing: we are to ensure that those who labour in the house of God do not go hungry because of their work.

> *"Bring the whole tithe into the storehouse, that there may be food in my house. Test me in this, says the Lord Almighty."*
>
> Malachi 3:10; cf. Deuteronomy 26:12

(2) We tithe so that, as in Old Testament times, the people of God can assemble in the presence of God and "rejoice" in everything that He has blessed them with.

> *"But you are to seek the place the Lord your God will choose from among all your tribes to put His Name there for His dwelling. To that place you must go; there bring your burnt offerings and sacrifices, **your** tithes and special gifts, what you have vowed to give and your freewill offerings [...]. There, in the presence of the Lord your God, you and your families shall eat and shall rejoice in everything you have put your hand to, because the Lord your God has blessed you."*
>
> Deuteronomy 12:5 ff.; cf. verses 11 ff.

(3) We tithe in order that, as the people of God, we may learn to revere him constantly.

Bringing the tithe (a tenth of our income) into the house of God shows that we have understood God's ways and His ordinances and that is a pointer towards the sincerity of our worship and our desire to obey His Word. In fact, offering the tithe to God is a wonderful way of expressing our gratitude and appreciation to Him for His tender mercy and His loving kindness towards us.

> *"Be sure to set aside a tenth of all that your fields produce each year. Eat the tithe of your grain, new wine and oil, and the firstborn of your herds and flocks in the presence of the Lord your God at the place He will choose as a dwelling for His Name, so that you may learn to revere the Lord your God always."*
> Deuteronomy 14:22 ff.

From these verses we learn that tithing is not only a matter of bringing money or other provisions into the house of God; it is also a way that God has appointed for us to learn to revere Him all the days of our lives.

In fact, tithing is a sign that we already revere the Lord. Personally, I am convinced that consistency in tithing is one of the most reliable indicators of Christian maturity. A Christian who regularly brings tithes and offerings into the local church demonstrates thereby that he already knows something of the fear of God. We should, of course, bear in mind that in the Bible the "fear of God" is simply equivalent to revering, honouring and respecting God. There is no suggestion of craven fear in the New Testament: "For you did not receive a spirit that makes you a slave again to fear" (Romans 8:15). "God did not give us a spirit of timidity, but a spirit of power, of love and of self-discipline" (2. Timothy 1:7).

Timidity and a craven spirit are two things with which we as Christians want to have nothing to do. Reverential fear, on the other hand, is a virtue that should be studied and practised by disciples of Jesus, who was "heard because of His reverent submission" (Hebrews 5:7). Tithing has shown itself again and again to be a unique way of practising the fear of God.

> *"Be sure to set aside a tenth of all that your fields produce each year. Eat the tithe of your grain, new wine and oil [...] in the presence of the Lord your God at the place He will choose as a dwelling for His Name, so that you may learn to revere the Lord your God always."*
>
> Deuteronomy 14:22 ff.

The Bible says, "The fear of the Lord is the beginning of knowledge" (Proverbs 1:7). Since tithing is learning how to revere or fear God, we could draw the conclusion that consistent tithing is the very beginning of the knowledge of God. Anyone who claims to know God ought, on that reckoning, to be a consistent contributor of tithes to his local assembly and not just a casual giver of a few coins into a "collection."

CHAPTER 5

WHERE SHOULD THE TITHE BE BROUGHT?

All Christians are called to belong to a gathering of believers where the Word of God is held to be the final and absolute authority. First and foremost, we are to bring the tithe to the place where God has called us to worship Him, the local church or assembly. This can be deduced from the instructions given to the people of Israel under the Old Covenant:

> *"You are to seek the place the Lord your God will choose from among all your tribes to put His name there for His dwelling. To that place you must go; there bring [...]* **your** *tithes and special gifts, what you have vowed to give and your freewill offerings [...]."*
> Deuteronomy 12:5 f.; cf. chapter 14:22-26

It is at the church or assembly, the gathering place of God's people, that the tithes should be released into the Lord's storehouse where they are to be used to support the ministry, to enable evangelism and to encourage missionary work.

> *"Bring the whole tithe into the storehouse."*
> Malachi 3:10a

Caution to Christians Who Have Emigrated

The following section is written primarily for Christian believers who have moved from their native countries to other lands and settled down to live there.

If the kind of church you attended previously or the denomination you belonged to is not to be found in your new country of residence, God's Word encourages you to seek carefully for the right place of worship in that country. It is of paramount importance that you find a church or an assembly, where Jesus Christ is recognized as the Son of God and where His death and resurrection are unquestioningly accepted and preached as the key to salvation. It is at such a church or assembly that you should offer the tithe and voluntary offerings.

The Scripture warns immigrants not to do what seems right in their own eyes. Instead, they are to obey God and to rely on Him for His leading in their new place of residence.

The four "ifs"

There are four "ifs" which will help you adapt and adjust your way of acting and thinking (with regard to tithing) to the new environment in which you find yourself.

1. If it was your custom to bring the tithe at the end of every month in your former church, and the pastor in your new place of worship asks his congregational members to bring the tithes at the beginning of the month, do not murmur at this request or be grieved because it differs from your former custom. In the end, it does not matter whether we bring the tithe at the end of the month or at the beginning — in both cases, we have to trust God to provide and act in faith through our giving. I would, however, suggest that you have a frank discussion with the pastor about this whole matter. If his heart is right before God, he will not make a big issue out of this.

2. If it has been your custom to use a part of the tithe to support your loved ones in your former church, you may find that this practise is not understood in your new place of worship. Many Christian churches teach that it is a Christian duty to bring "the whole tithe" into the storehouse, and that is, as we have seen, exactly what God's Word teaches. Ideally, therefore, you should bring the tithes and offerings to the church which you now attend and not to a church which you once attended and have now left. However, I am sure that a local church minister whose heart is right before God will not insist on this, if it means that you have to stop supporting the poor and needy in your home country. Of course, if you have a fixed source of income in your new country, the perfect solution would be either for you to bring the tithe to your local assembly and send freewill offerings back to your former home country, or for you to get your local church so interested in your former country that the leadership is willing to join you in supporting the people there. God's Word encourages not only individual believers to tithe but also whole assemblies. There are many examples of fine Christian churches in Europe who give a tithe of their income and more to missionary work and to the support of poor Christians in other lands. God has richly blessed them for this.

3. If, in your former church, it was no problem for you to keep back a part of the tithe in times of financial need or crisis, but you become aware that this is not approved of in your new place of worship, then you would need to seek the face of the Lord for *wisdom*. God promises to honour those who honour Him, and if you have been giving regularly and generously, you should normally expect Him to bless you richly. Could it be that there is some sin in your life that is blocking the flow of God's blessing? Or could it be that God is bringing you into a difficult situation to make you realize how much you need to depend on Him in all things and sometimes, even on your Christian brothers and sisters for material support? Perhaps the situation requires you to seek counselling and perhaps even financial help from the leadership of your church. If their hearts are right before the Lord, they will be only too glad to do what they can to assist you in these circumstances. There are, again, fine Christian churches in Europe where members of the oversight are prepared to take the time and trouble to help you order your financial affairs in such a way as to set you free from debt.

On the other hand, if you have the impression that rules about tithing are more important to your pastor than your personal welfare, then perhaps you are not in the right church after all. Beware of spiritual abuse! A local church is a place where you can love and be loved with all your strengths and all your weaknesses. If rules and expectations, particularly concerning money, are used to put pressure on you to conform or to force you to act against what you know in your heart is right before God, then the sooner you leave that church the better it will be for you and your soul! Never forget that God loves a "cheerful giver", it is voluntary, willing obedience that God is looking for in you, not the slavish obedience of someone who is afraid to stand up for his convictions!

4. If you have been accustomed to asking your local church for a loan and expecting it to be granted because you have been tithing, you need to know that this is a thoroughly unscriptural practise. Money that is given is offered to the Lord. The local church is responsible to Him for the way it is used, and the Bible does not speak anywhere of giving tithes back as a loan. If you need a loan, you should normally go to an accredited bank and apply for it there, the same way as everyone else does. Let me say this quite clearly: When you put money in a collection-plate or offering-box, you are giving it away to the Lord Jesus for Him to use. From that moment on, you have no more claim to that money. The fact that you gave a donation to a church neither entitles you to loans and other special treatment, nor does it give you the right to determine church policy or take influence on the leadership. Attempting to do this is a form of blackmail and is evidence of lack of spirituality.

> *"You are not to do as we do here today [i.e. before crossing the Jordan and migrating to the new land], everyone as he sees fit, since you have not yet reached the resting place and the inheritance the Lord your God is giving you. But you will cross the Jordan and settle in the land the Lord your God is giving you as an inheritance, and He will give you rest from all your enemies around you so that you will live in safety. Then to the place the Lord your God will choose as a dwelling for His Name — there you are to bring everything I command you: your burnt offerings and sacrifices, **your** tithes and special gifts, and all the choice possessions you have vowed to the Lord."*
> Deuteronomy 12:8-11; cf. chapter 26:1-3

The believer who has permanently emigrated from his homeland to another, often finds himself in a difficult situation. His loyalty to the assembly or movement he has left behind makes him want to find something similar in his new country, but often there is simply nothing quite like it. And unless he is called to establish a church on the principles he has learned, he will have to learn to adapt to the new situation and find his footing in a local church or assembly that is a little different from the one he has left behind. This process will take time, in some cases many years, and unfortunately I cannot promise that it will always be without a great deal of pain and inner conflict. But as Christians, we know that we are called of God to be a part of the local gathering of believers, and so we will do our utmost best to join in and support its activities, even when we feel that some things ought to be done differently.

In many towns and cities in Europe, there are a large number of churches to choose from. In such cases, it is important to seek the Lord as to which is the right one for you. As an evangelical believer, I feel strongly that it is important to find a Bible-believing, Bible-preaching church where experiences such as conversion, the new birth and the fullness of the Holy Spirit are at the very least accepted and preferably preached and practised. It is only in a church like this that a believer can really tithe in faith, knowing that his gifts will be used for the furtherance of the Gospel. It is a sad fact that there are many so-called "churches" around, where the Gospel is rarely preached, if at all, and where the power of God's Word has been replaced by a power-less theology that puts more emphasis on social and political action than on the exposition of Bible truth or the practise of true Christian fellowship. Sometimes Christian believers from other countries join such churches, thinking that they will change them through their influence and example. But more often than not, it is not the church that is changed but the believer. If you have left your home country for another, I therefore strongly advise you to look around for a church or an assembly that upholds the Word of God and at the same time practises the love of Jesus. There are more such churches around than many people think!

Above all, remember that God is good and wants you to be blessed.

> *"Dear friend, I pray that you may enjoy good health and that all may go well with you, even as your soul is getting along well."*
>
> 3. John 1:2

In particular, God wants you to bear fruit in your life, thus promoting His glory and your own well-being. But how much less will the fruit in your life be if you choose the wrong church and get involved with people whose heart and mind are not directed towards Him! And what fruit can your tithing bear if you are donating money to a church that makes no difference between the cause of the Gospel and the cause of a lukewarm, watered-down theology? My friend, it is for your own good that I quote again from Scripture:

> *"Be careful not to sacrifice your burnt offerings anywhere you please. Offer them only at the place the Lord will choose."*
> Deuteronomy 12:13 ff.

If you are a Christian from abroad looking for a church in your new place of residence, you may expect the Lord to help you to find a church or assembly where you will be loved and accepted, where you can practise at least some of the gifts God has given you, and where you can bring the tithes and offerings with a clear conscience.

CHAPTER 6

THE RECIPIENTS OF THE TITHE AND ITS USE

Who Should Receive The Tithe?

The Levites

In the Old Testament times, the Levites were a priestly family who were entitled to receive the tithes of the people of God. In the New Testament times, it is the leadership or oversight of the local church or assembly who are to be the recipients of believers' tithes and offerings.

In his last words to his twelve sons, the patriarch Jacob cursed two of them, namely Simeon and Levi, because they killed a man and hamstrung (i.e. lamed or paralysed) oxen in their fierce anger. Simeon and Levi were so violent that their father, Jacob, could not bring them under control. And this is what Jacob said to the two of them on his death bed:

> *"Simeon and Levi are brothers — their swords are weapons of violence. Let me not enter their council, let me not join their assembly, for they have killed men in their anger and hamstrung oxen as they pleased. Cursed be their anger, so fierce, and their fury, so cruel! I will scatter them in Jacob and disperse them in Israel."*
>
> Genesis 49:5 ff.

Simeon and his descendants were dispersed by being absorbed into the tribe of Judah. They lived in the area allotted to Judah (Joshua 15:20-63; 19:1-9). Levi and his descendants however, rose to prominence because they were the first tribe to return to God after the golden calf incident. Thereafter they were chosen by God to offer sacrifices and perform special priestly services. This is what the Lord said to Moses about the Levites:

> *"I have taken the Levites from among the Israelites in place of the first male offspring of every Israelite woman. The Levites are Mine."*
>
> Numbers 3:12

When Moses blessed the tribes of Israel shortly before his death, he distinguished the Levites by offering up a quite remarkable intercessory prayer for them:

> *"About Levi he said: 'Your Thummim [perfections] and Urim [light] belong to the man you favoured. [...] He teaches Your precepts to Jacob and Your law to Israel. He offers incense before You and whole burnt offerings on Your altar. Bless all his skills, O Lord, and be pleased with the work of his hands."*
>
> Deuteronomy 33:8,10-11

Although Levi had previously been cursed by his father Jacob, his descendants were afterwards redeemed from the curse because the Lord was gracious to them and because Moses prayed for them. The Levites were spared, having to bear the consequences of the curse no longer. However, they did not inherit a fixed portion of the promised land of Canaan when this was later divided among the tribes of Israel. Instead, they were allotted a number of priestly cities to live in; and their income was to be from Israel's tithes. The Israelites were commanded to give a tenth of all they produced to the tribe of Levi. God instructed them expressly:

> *"I give to the Levites all the tithes in Israel as their inheritance in return for the work they do while serving at the Tent of Meeting. [...] It is the Levites who are*

> *to do the work at the Tent of Meeting and bear the responsibility for offences against it. [...] They will receive no inheritance among the Israelites. Instead, I give to the Levites as their inheritance the tithes that the Israelites present as an offering to the Lord. That is why I said concerning them: 'They will have no inheritance among the Israelites.'"*
>
> Numbers 18:21-24

The Bible says that the people of God agreed to obey God's commandment and that, as a consequence, they brought the first of their produce, their offerings and the tithes to the storerooms of the house of God, where they were given to the Levites (Nehemiah 10:37).

The Bible tells us that the Old Testament Scriptures are examples that were written for our learning and in order to warn and help us (1. Corinthians 10:11). They still have a meaning for today's church. It is true that the old covenant has been replaced by the new, but under this new dispensation we may and should learn from what happened to the people of God in the ancient times. Under the new covenant, all believers are called to be "priests" under Jesus Christ, because He has made a priestly caste unnecessary by offering His blood on the Cross once and for all. But that does not mean that there is no more service to be done.

The New Testament speaks frequently of ministries, of pastors and shepherds, of elders or presbyters, of teachers and preachers, and of evangelists, whose task is to go out to the world and preach the saving Gospel of Jesus Christ. Some do this in their spare time, often working extremely hard to support themselves without being a financial burden to those they minister to. Their self-sacrifice is praiseworthy and will one day receive a great reward. However, the New Testament makes it plain that there is such a thing as a full-time ministry, and that it is the will of God that the men and women who are called to such a ministry should be supported by the churches they serve. It is my conviction that God has instituted tithing in his New Testament church in order to make such a ministry possible. First and foremost, the tithes of church members are given to support the ministry of the local church. Every other need is to be subordinated to this.

As God assigned the tithe to the Levites in the Old Testament so that they could perform their ministry without worrying about what they were to live on, so he has ordained tithing in the New Testament church in order that pastors and other ministers can be paid an appropriate wage and can perform their ministry without having to worry about the things of daily life. There is a passage in Paul's first letter to Timothy which makes this particularly clear:

> *"The elders who direct the affairs of the church well are worthy of double honour,*

> *especially those whose work is preaching and teaching. For the Scripture says, 'Do not muzzle the ox while it is treading out the grain,' and 'The worker deserves his wages.'"*
>
> 1. Timothy 5:17 ff.

Whichever way you choose to interpret "double honour" it is obvious that God intends that those who give themselves to full-time spiritual service in His kingdom should reap an earthly harvest of wages, drawn from the tithes and offerings given to the local church by its members. This is exactly the same principle as was applied to the Levites in the Old Testament.

> *"Moreover, we will bring to the storerooms of the house of our God [...] the first of our ground meal, of our grain offerings, of the fruit of all our trees and of our new wine and oil. And we will bring a tithe of our crops to the Levites, for it is the Levites who collect the tithes in all the towns where we work. A priest descended from Aaron is to accompany the Levites when they receive the tithes, and the Levites are to bring a tenth of the tithes up to the house of our God, to the storerooms of the treasury."*
>
> Nehemiah 10:37 ff.

There are three wonderful principles which can be learnt from this passage from Nehemiah. Firstly, the people of God willingly brought the tithes and offerings to the Levites both for their support and for the support of the house of God. Secondly, the Levites were held accountable for what they received: an Aaronic priest was to watch over their work and to see that everything was done as God had commanded. There was no chance for any Levite to run off with temple funds or to misuse the tithes that had been entrusted to his care in any other way. In today's churches it is important that pastors and other ministers are accountable to the church for the money that they collect and that church treasurers or other officers are appointed to watch over the use of church funds and to ensure that everything is done honestly and faithfully. And thirdly, the Levites themselves were expected to tithe what they themselves received. Ministers who are paid a wage from tithes and offerings are themselves not exempt from the Christian duty of tithing. They, too, should be seen to be giving a tenth of their income towards the work of the local assembly or of their denomination.

The Foreigner, the Widow and the Fatherless

The tithes of God's people were not given exclusively to the Levites. Far from it. Tithes and offerings were also used to support philanthropic activities, by which I mean helping people less well-off than oneself. The congregation was commanded to bring tithes and offerings for the benefit of those who had no income of their own.

> *"When you have finished setting aside a tenth of all your produce in the third year, the year of the tithe, you shall give it to the Levite, the alien, the fatherless and the widow, so that they may eat in your towns and be satisfied."*
>
> Deuteronomy 26:12

Caution to believers

As we have just seen, the tithe was not used exclusively to support ministers, but was also distributed to the foreigner, the fatherless and the widow. In a large, thriving assembly there will be more than enough money coming in through the willing gifts of the members to support the minister and to do good to others. This is the ideal situation. But unfortunately, the ideal is not always available. In many small churches, the income from tithes and offerings is barely enough to support the minister. In such cases, it is good to bear in mind that the Levites were the initial recipients of the tithe. To put it in New Testament terms, a Christian congregation can only afford to give generously to the needy if it is still able to offer its own minister adequate support. The minister's wages should be first on its list of priorities.

> *"I give to the Levites all the tithes in Israel as their inheritance in return for*

> *the work they do while serving at the Tent of Meeting. [...] I give to the Levites as their inheritance the tithes that the Israelites present as an offering to the Lord."*
>
> Numbers 18:21-24

Money matters can be a great cause of controversy within Christian churches. In order to avoid the problems and heartbreaks that can accompany this whole subject, it is important that absolute transparency in church finances is there or present. Elders and other church officers should keep strict accounts. The pastor's wages should be agreed upon by the eldership (if they are not already determined by denominational policy,) and it should be understood that these wages should be paid regularly and have priority over any other use of church income. The church leadership can then agree on a month-by-month basis on how to best dispose of any money that is left over. I do not wish to be controversial here, but I wonder if some churches would be more successful and begin to grow if they supported their minister more and worried less about maintaining a magnificent church building. The church of Jesus Christ is about people, not about buildings. A beautiful church meeting-room is a luxury; a minister who is set free to preach God's Word without the pressure of daily care is a necessity.

What To Do When You Have Given The Tithe

Make a confession of faith. The Scripture says:

> *"If you confess with your mouth, 'Jesus is Lord,' and believe in your heart that God raised him from the dead, you will be saved. For it is with your heart that you believe and are justified, and it is with your mouth that you confess and are saved."*
>
> Romans 10:9 ff.

Verbal confession is a means of expressing your faith and of achieving victory — victory over the sins of stinginess and rapacity, victory over debt and victory over the devourer. Jesus said that if you believe you can also tell mountains to be removed from your way. But you cannot confess that you have the victory until you have believed absolutely in what you are saying. There is no truthful, effective confession unless there is real faith in our hearts.

Jesus once said to His disciples,

> *"I tell you the truth, if anyone says to this mountain, 'Go, throw yourself into the sea,' and does not doubt in his heart, but believes that what he says will happen, it will be done for him."*
>
> Mark 11:23

And Moses gave the following wise advice to the Israelites:

"When you have finished setting aside a tenth of all your produce in the third year, the year of the tithe, you shall give it to the Levite, the alien, the fatherless and the widow, so that they may eat in your towns and be satisfied. Then say to the Lord your God [here you can agree with Moses in this prayer]: 'I have removed from my house the sacred portion and have given it to the Levite, the alien, the fatherless and the widow, according to all you commanded. I have not turned aside from your commands nor have I forgotten any of them. I have not eaten any of the sacred portion while I was in mourning, nor have I removed any of it while I was unclean, nor have I offered any of it to the dead. I have obeyed the Lord my God; I have done everything you commanded me. Look down from heaven, your holy dwelling-place, and bless your people Israel and the land you have given us as you promised on oath to our forefathers, a land flowing with milk and honey.'"

Deuteronomy 26:12-15

When you have handed over the tithe to the local church, it is wise and scriptural to pray and make a confession such as that outlined in Deuteronomy 26:12-15. Make a verbal confession of your faith and obedience before God in prayer. You might like to use the following pattern when you pray:

> **"Lord, I have removed the tithe from my house and given it gladly to the church as you have commanded; I have been obedient to your commandment and have not forgotten it.**
> **I have not used any of it for my own selfish purposes, nor have I given any part of it to the spiritually dead.**
> **In Your grace, please make these offerings of mine a blessing to our congregation. In particular, I ask You to pour out spiritual and material blessings on our minister and on all who faithfully serve this congregation. I ask this in the Name of my Lord and Saviour Jesus Christ.**
> **Lord, please also look down from heaven and bless my own house and family for Your Name's sake. Amen."**

Try to keep to this simple scriptural pattern. It will help you to confess and strengthen your faith after you have faithfully brought the tithe into God's storehouse.

How the Tithe Should Be Used

1. As we have already learnt from the previous chapters, tithes are first and foremost used to

support the legitimate full-time ministry. That is why God said:

"Bring the whole tithe into the storehouse, that there may be food in My house."
Malachi 3:10

This means that God wants there to be enough resources and support in the local church for His ministers as well as for the needy.

"He ordered the people living in Jerusalem to give the portion due to the priests and Levites so that they could devote themselves to the Law of the Lord. [...] When Hezekiah and his officials came and saw the heaps, they praised the Lord and blessed His people Israel. Hezekiah asked the priests and Levites about the heaps; and Azariah the chief priest, from the family of Zadok, answered, 'Since the people began to bring their contributions to the temple of the Lord, we have had enough to eat and plenty to spare, because the Lord has blessed His people, and this great amount is left over.'"
2. Chronicles 31:4; 8-10; cf. Nehemiah 13:10 ff.

2. Tithes should also be used to enable philanthropic activities, which basically means meeting the needs of the alien and of impoverished widows and orphans, the goal being that they might praise the Lord for His abundant mercy and provision.

> *"Then say to the Lord your God, 'I have removed from my house the sacred portion and have given it to the Levite, the alien, the fatherless and the widow, so that they may eat [...] and be satisfied."*
> Deuteronomy 26:13; cf. chapter 14:27 ff.

CHAPTER 7

THE CONSEQUENCES OF ABSTAINING FROM TITHING

When the members of the Body of Christ abstain from tithing, the following results may be expected:

1. Those called to do full-time ministry may suffer from hunger and from various other pressing problems (see Malachi 3:10). Ministers are human beings like everyone else and have the same basic needs as the members of their congregation. It is very logical that if their basic needs are left unmet, their ministry will suffer. And if their ministry suffers, obviously those church members towards whom this ministry is directed also suffer. Thus we see that church members who abstain from tithing not only harm their ministers but themselves too.

In the Old Testament, both Azariah, the chief priest from the house of Zadok, and the entire priestly family were forced to go hungry when the people of God refused or simply forgot to tithe.

> *"And Azariah the chief priest, from the family of Zadok, answered, 'Since the people began to bring their contributions to the temple of the Lord, we have had enough to eat and plenty to spare, because the Lord has blessed His people, and this great amount is left over."*
>
> 2. Chronicles 31:10

Of course God could have performed a miracle to supply the priests with food and everything else they needed. But He did not, and His Word indicates that in most situations it is His will for His ministers to be provided for through the regular giving activity of His people:

> *"And do not neglect the Levites living in your towns, for they have no allotment or inheritance of their own. At the end of every three years, bring all the tithes of that year's produce and store it in your towns, so that the Levites (who have no allotment or inheritance of their own) and the aliens, the fatherless and the widows who live in your towns may come and eat and be satisfied, and so that the Lord your*

God may bless you in all the work of your hands."

Deuteronomy 14:27 ff.

2. The philanthropic activities of the church, and here I would include evangelistic outreach (i.e. helping the needy and organizing crusades etc.), may break down for lack of funds. The tithes given by church members are used to support the needy and for the work of the church in general. A lack of income has a debilitating effect on the Lord's work and may mean that people in need do not receive the assistance which a local church might otherwise be able to provide.

"When you have finished setting aside a tenth of all your produce [...], you shall give it to the Levite, the alien, the fatherless and the widow, so that they may eat in your towns and be satisfied."

Deuteronomy 26:12

3. It may well be that godly ministers get discouraged or even see themselves forced to resign from their leadership position and take up secular work in order to be able to survive. There is a sad example of this phenomenon to be found in the Old Testament book of Nehemiah:

> *"I also learned that the portions assigned to the Levites had not been given to them, and that all the Levites and singers responsible for the service had gone back to their own fields. So I rebuked the officials and asked them, 'Why is the house of God neglected?' Then I called them together and stationed them at their posts."*
>
> Nehemiah 13:10 ff.

4. Certain other ministers may decide to stay in the ministry, yet their hearts may grow cold and their ministry become superficial. Due to the constant lack to which they are subjected and the care and stress that this brings with it, their dedication to the Lord's work suffers and the anointing on their work is considerably impeded.

Others may be led astray by their own ego to manipulate younger members of the church into giving more than God's Word warrants in order to obtain what they so ardently desire. This can cause much heartache and has been known to destroy the faith of young people who started their walk with the Lord full of faith, hope and love but were then hopelessly overburdened by an ambitious but ill-advised minister.

When, however, God's people faithfully bring the tithe into God's storehouse, these spiritual dangers are avoided, thus promoting both the natural and the spiritual welfare of ministers and churches alike. Tithing has been ordained for the express purpose of enabling chosen men and women to devote themselves to studying and teaching God's precious Word, the result being that all the members of the church benefit.

> *"He (King Hezekiah) ordered the people living in Jerusalem to give the portion due to the priests and Levites so that they could devote themselves to the Law of the Lord."*
>
> 2. Chronicles 31:4

When God's people are reluctant to give and to support their ministers, this makes it very difficult for those ministers on their part to minister faithfully to the spiritual and physical needs of their church members. One often hears people complaining about their minister's lack of dedication, well prepared sermons, time for counselling purposes etc., but I wonder if these complaints are not simply the fruit of an unwillingness to give to the Lord's work.

In young charismatic or neo-Pentecostal churches, in particular, it is often the case that a young minister will take great sacrifices on himself to build up a congregation in the face of opposition from more traditional church leaders. But such sacrifices should not be expected of such men, and certainly not for many years without end. Keeping your minister poor is probably the best way to rob him of his anointing and rob your church of the blessing it once enjoyed.

If we want our pastors or ministers to be joyful, outgoing and dependent on the Lord, the best thing we can do for them, is to make sure that they see their prayers answered and their needs met. If we do our part in bringing the tithe into the local church, we may find that in the course of time we no longer have reason to complain that our ministers have no time for us or for the tasks they have really been called to do. But if we neglect to bring the tithes into the local assembly and despise the Christian ministry of giving, then we do not have to be surprised when our ministers seem demotivated, discouraged or even distrustful. I am not saying that this is right or spiritual, but it is perfectly natural. God has ordained that His ministers be taken care of through the gifts of His people, and if we as His people do not give, ministers will suffer and may even question God's calling on their lives.

When this happens such ministers should under no circumstances be accused of 'carnality'. This would not be true, for it is God the Holy Spirit who has ordained the principle of sowing and reaping, giving and receiving, and this principle is still in force in the church today. When believers contribute generously to the support of local ministers, they may expect that these ministers will then rejoice in the blessing received and return it manifoldly to their congregation in the form of heartfelt, encouraging preaching.

It is high time for the Body of Christ to recognize this godly principle of generosity, and to honour the ministers of God in the way that the Bible teaches from beginning to end. If even the Old Testament teaches the need to support ministers, how much more the New!

> *"For the lips of a priest should preserve knowledge, and from his mouth people should seek instruction — because he is the messenger of the Lord Almighty."*
> Malachi 2:7

The Bible encourages the idea that there should be an exchange between those who share their spiritual experiences and knowledge and those who regularly receive this instruction.

> *"Anyone who receives instruction in the word must share all good things with his instructor."*
> Galatians 6:6

The ministers of the gospel of Christ should never be treated as hirelings, but as God's servants or messengers whose labour in His vineyard makes them worthy of remuneration. The Scripture says quite expressly that ministers of the gospel deserve 'double honour' and that their needs are to be cared for by the local congregation of believers. It is the responsibility of God's people to fulfil this noble calling by bringing the tithe into God's storehouse and giving "as to the Lord."

He will then keep His promise and "throw open the floodgates of heaven and pour out so much blessing that you will not have room enough for it" (Malachi 3:10).

CHAPTER 8

GOD'S PROMISES TO FAITHFUL TITHERS

It is God who supplies the farmer with seed to sow and who gives us all bread for food. His resources are endless, and a child of God needs to understand that God is more than able to fulfil every promise that He has ever made. The Bible testifies plainly that "He who promised is faithful" (Hebrews 10:23) and cannot lie.

> *"God, who does not lie, promised before the beginning of time."*
>
> Titus 1:2

God has faithfully promised to bless those cheerful, generous givers who bring the tithes and offerings into His storehouse. Let us list some of the blessings that (according to Malachi 3:10ff.) will ensue when we begin to tithe:

(1) God will open the windows of heaven for our benefit and blessing. God will never — I repeat NEVER — be a debtor to man. If we bring the tithe and offerings faithfully into His house, He will pour out spiritual blessings more abundantly than we are able to ask or think. Not because we deserve them, but because He wants to show us how much more munificent He is than we could ever be. Praise His Name!

(2) God will grant us protection against "pests". In the pictorial language of the Old Testament, this means those forces that would "devour our crops" — in plain New Testament language, the Satanic enemy who goes around seeking to destroy our life, our marriage, our children, our business, our finances and our health. God promises to prevent his onslaughts, when we faithfully bring the tithes to Him.

If you are a "cheerful giver", (2. Corinthians 9:7) God has promised to arise on your behalf as a "mighty man of war", divinely intervening to prevent the enemy from laying waste to the fruit He wants to produce in your life; you may rest assured that the Lord Himself is watching over your life *"to increase your store of seed and [...] enlarge the harvest of your righteousness"* (2. Corinthians 9:10). *"You will be made rich in every way so that you can be generous on every occasion"* (2. Corinthians 9:11).

Barrenness, poverty and fruitlessness will be things of the past. Your willing obedience to God and His Word, and your genuine willingness to give back to God what belongs to Him, bring the promises of God into operation. God will now act on your behalf. You will now have the opportunity to witness His faithfulness in action, the fulfilment of His unfailing promises.

Through the prophet Malachi God said,

"Bring the whole tithe into the storehouse, that there may be food in My house. Test Me in this, says the Lord Almighty, and see:
- *if I will not throw open the floodgates of heaven*
- *and pour out so much blessing that you will not have room enough for it.*
- *I will prevent pests from devouring your crops,*
- *and the vines in your fields will not cast their fruit, says the Lord Almighty. [This is God's promise of protection against barrenness and fruitlessness.]*
- *Then all the nations will call you blessed, for yours will be a delightful land, says the Lord Almighty"* (Malachi 3:10 ff.).

Tithing is one of the most crucial issues in God's plan to bless His people. God deliberately states here that He wants us to test Him in this matter. For as soon as we begin to tithe, God regards it as a point of honour to fulfill His covenant promises towards us. That is why this is an especially valuable promise for those who lack faith

in God's willingness to do for them what He has stated in His Word. God gives them something practical to do which elicits an immediate response from Him. As soon as they act on His Word, God responds to bless them, thus increasing their faith and their ability to believe in all the other Biblical promises.

As we see from the Scripture quoted above, tithes and offerings are God-given golden keys to unlock the windows of heaven and cause the abundance of God's manifold blessing to be poured out into our life, marriage, family, business, ministry, and so on.

Tithes and offerings are linked to specific promises. If we make faithful and regular contributions to His storehouse and, at the same time, believe in these promises, we can expect God to act on our behalf in preventing the devil from robbing us of the fruits of our faith through his pestilential influence on our marriage, children, business, finances or church.

Biblical tithing is effectual in the sight of God and causes Him to arise from His rest and defend the faithful, obedient and cheerful giver. God promises to prevent spiritual pestilence in the life of the generous giver.

Sometimes we pray earnestly and even fast in order to overcome the attacks of the devil, but if we are faithful in giving tithes and offerings, we may rest confident that God is on our side and that our prayers are heard even before we verbalize them. We could put this another way. We know that Satan flees when we resist him by faith. But what better way exists to resist Satan than to submit ourselves to God in this matter of bringing the whole tithe into His storehouse?[3]

In Ecclesiastes we read:

> *"Guard your steps when you go to the house of God. Go near to listen rather than to offer the sacrifice of fools, who do not know that they do wrong."*
> Ecclesiastes 5:1

We must realize that when tithes and offerings are faithfully brought into the Lord's storehouse, God will undertake to bless both the congregation and its minister(s). Failure to submit to God's will, however, renders us defenceless and enables that "roaring lion," the devil, to seek us out as his prey and devour us (1. Peter 5:8).

---

[3] cf. James 4:7.

Tithes and Offerings

Up to this point, we have been studying the promises of God with regard to "tithing". In the last few paragraphs, however, we have spoken of "tithes and offerings". These two expressions occur together so often in the Scripture that we can safely assume that they really do belong together. In Old Testament times, the people of God not only brought the tithes to God, but also added a number of freewill offerings. As a case in point, we should turn to Malachi 3:8, where God asks His people, "Will a man rob God? Yet you rob me." The people ask in response, "How do we rob You?" And God replies very firmly, "In tithes and offerings." God expected His Old Testament people not only to bring the "whole tithe" into His storehouse, but also to add freewill offerings. Only when they did this, then they did show that their heart was right before Him.

By tithing we prove our obedience to God, but it is the addition of offerings by which we can best express our love to God and our desire that His kingdom should thrive. Offerings indicate our willingness to go beyond the strict letter of the law of God on tithing; they are, so to speak, a down-payment on our willingness to offer everything we have and everything we are to the One who has redeemed us for time and eternity. When we bring an additional offering above and beyond the tithe, we are telling God in the most practical way possible that we owe our life and our all to Him and that we are eternally grateful for all that He has done for us, is doing for us and will continue to do for us till the end of time.

In this sense we could say that *tithing* is a Christian duty and an act of obedience, whilst *freewill offerings* show that we are not only prepared to obey God but also to love and serve Him with all our being. In the end, both tithing and giving freewill offerings are ways of honouring God, and we know from His "great and precious promises" that, *"Those who honour me I will honour" (2. Peter 1:4; 1. Samuel 2:30).*

Tithes are not a substitute for offerings, nor are offerings a substitute for tithing. Ideally, we should be giving the tithes and freewill offerings besides. Never try to substitute one for the other, for God has appointed them both as part of His divine ordering of the church.

> *"You rob Me [...] in tithes and in offerings."*
>
> Malachi 3:8

It would be pointless and senseless even to attempt to replace tithing with offerings or vice-versa. God's Word is quite clear on this and attaches wonderful promises of blessing to both.

So let the floodgates of heaven be opened for you as you faithfully bring the tithe into your local assembly; and let all spiritual blessings in heavenly places be poured out upon you until you are unable to contain them as you cheerfully and gladly bring your offerings into the Lord's storehouse.

CHAPTER 9

THE NEGATIVE RESULTS OF FAILING TO TITHE

Retributive Judgement

In the power of God's anointing, Moses, God's prophet, spoke and set the Levites free from the curse of their forefather Jacob. First, he asked God to bless them in their work. Then he prayed the following words:

> *"Strike the loins of those who rise against him [the tribe of Levi]; strike his foes till they rise no more."*
> Deuteronomy 33:11b

Moses asked the Lord to afflict the "loins" of those who would rise up to hinder Levi in his priestly work. In the Bible, the word "loins" is an euphemism for the reproductive organs.

Moses' declaration contains a warning for all those who bring false charges against the Lord's servants. The fact that so many Christians today live a spiritually unfruitful life could in some way be linked to the way they treat and talk about God's servants. The Bible says that an undeserved curse does not come to rest. But it seems obvious to me that many believers have been struck by God because of their wrong attitude, the consequence being that their spiritual life is barren and that their churches are shrinking rather than growing. It is true that God's servants, being human, make their mistakes, just like anyone else. But if a man or woman has followed God's call on his or her life to serve him, there needs to be an adequate cause before anyone lays obstacles in their path. Criticizing ministers without an adequate reason and thereby damaging their reputation in the church or even outside of it, is something that believers should beware not to do, if not for the sake of common decency, then to avoid endangering themselves. God guards the honour of his servants like the apple of his eye. Moses' prophecy about Levi still applies, in a spiritual sense, today. For the Bible says,

> *"Not the smallest letter, not the least stroke of a pen, will by any means disappear from the Law until everything is accomplished."*
>
> Matthew 5:18

And again,

> *"Do not let your mouth lead you into sin. And do not protest to the [temple] messenger, 'My vow was a mistake.' Why should God be angry at what you say and destroy the work of your hands?"*
>
> Ecclesiastes 5:6

To needlessly criticize your minister or impede him in his work because of some minor difference of opinion could be damaging to your spiritual life not to mention the heartache such things cause in Christian churches. Ministers are, on the whole, people who have sacrificed a successful secular career to follow the calling and anointing of God on their lives. We should respect this, knowing that God Himself is watching over them for good and not for evil. Fighting against such a "servant of God" is, in the end, the same as fighting that servant's God. *"The elders who direct the affairs of the church well are worthy of double honour, especially those whose work is teaching and preaching. [...] Do not entertain an accusation against an elder unless it is brought by two or three witnesses. Those who [do actually] sin are to be rebuked publicly, so that the others may take warning"* (1. Timothy 5:17,19-20).

In this passage from his First Letter to Timothy, Paul states quite clearly two things about ministers. One is that they are "worthy of double honour" and that accusations against them should not be brought lightly or without due justification. The other is that, if they do fall into grievous sin, this is a serious matter requiring church discipline such as to be rebuked publicly. If a minister falls into sin, this concerns the whole assembly. But if a minister is doing his best to serve God and does not fall into grievous sin, bringing minor or trumped-up accusations against him, would be the most counter-productive thing that anyone could do. It would be doing the work of the devil for him.

Making the lives of church leaders difficult seems to be a favourite hobby among some so-called "Spirit-filled" Christians. No wonder their lives are marked by defeat and retrogression and their churches by lack of power and introspection! How different many churches are from the Biblical ideal of a group of people working together with all their heart and soul to promote love and brotherly understanding and to preach the Gospel to the unsaved! This is the result of backsliding and disobedience. One of the clearest signs of backsliding in a Pentecostal church is the members' reluctance or downright refusal to bring the tithes and offerings into the Lord's storehouse. Yet God has said,

> *"A tithe of everything from the land, whether grain from the soil or fruit from the trees, belongs to the Lord; it is holy to the Lord."*
>
> Leviticus 27:30

Refusal to bring one's tithes and offerings into God's storehouse (the local church) should never, I repeat never, be used as a means to harm or blackmail the minister of a church. Although the Levites (God's ministers under the old covenant) were entitled to collect the Israelites' tithes and offerings, they themselves were not the initiators of the commandment on tithing. Rather, it was the Lord Himself who gave this commandment, and the tithe is described as holy to Him. Disobeying God by refusing to bring the tithe into His storehouse cannot therefore be the way to "punish" your minister if he has in some way offended you. If your minister has offended you, you should pray about it and, if you still feel wronged, talk to him, if necessary before witnesses. But you bring the tithes and offerings to God, not to the minister, and refusing to bring them into God's storehouse would be disobedience towards the Word of God itself. The way to be "happy in Jesus" is to "trust and obey" the Lord, no matter what your minister may have said or done to upset you.

God wants you to prosper and be in good physical and spiritual health. He has never intended a single defeat for you; instead, He wants you and your entire family to increase and abound in His rich peace and spiritual resources. The Bible says that God takes pleasure in our prosperity. That is to say, He is happy when it is well with you, with your family, children, business, finance, education, etc. God loves to bless His children. But if we deliberately flout His Word and disregard the instructions

He has given us for our good, we have only ourselves to blame if we do not prosper or do not enjoy His blessing.

Condemnation and Curse

Let us look again at what God said through the prophet Malachi. Israelites who refused to bring the tithe to the temple are described there as "thieves" or "robbers." Their motives obviously reflected avarice or stinginess; characteristics, which the Bible summarizes as "covetousness" and condemns as being the equivalent of idolatory.

The LORD asks with a view to tithing:

"Will a man rob God? Yet you rob Me. But you ask, How do we rob You? In tithes and offerings."

Malachi 3:8

A believer who deliberately deprives God of the tithe, is here charged with the sin of robbery. He or she is condemned in the sight of God as a covenant breaker, as someone infected with the spirit of greed, selfishness and covetousness. The tithes of believers belong to God, and when we withhold them from Him, we commit an act of theft.

It is a desire for pleasure and material gain that causes Christians to be avaricious. Unfortunately, many of those who started off well, having understood the principles of tithing, have ended up as robbers in the assemblies of God because of their greed and hunger for wealth. And although there may be many "good" excuses to justify their actions, God sees such people as covenant breakers as long as they neglect their commitment to tithe. In this context, it is not being unkind to say that they are stingy, greedy and unfaithful children of God, whose love for their own pleasure and welfare has led them astray and caused them to disrespect and disobey God.

As the Bible says in the Book of Malachi:

"A son honours his father and a servant his master. If I am a father, where is the honour due to me? If I am a master, where is the respect due to me? says the Lord Almighty..."

Malachi 1:6

"If I am a father, where is the honor due me? If I am a master, where is the respect due me?"

Mal. 1:6

"Bring the whole tithe into the storehouse, that there may be FOOD in my house."

Mal. 3:10

In this world, if someone is caught stealing, he is arrested, judged, and imprisoned for his deed. In the Kingdom of God, the consequences are equally dire, although they may not become immediately manifest. The one who robs God of the tenth, takes from Him that which rightfully belongs to Him and which is esteemed as holy (Leviticus 27:30). Is it any wonder that such a profane person becomes subject to a spiritual curse?

> *"You are under a curse — the whole nation of you — because you are robbing Me."*
>
> Malachi 3:9

If we take this Old Testament passage literally, we cannot escape the conclusion that God does in fact send a spiritual curse on all those who rob Him through withholding from Him and from His house the tithe that He has ordained to be brought there.

> *"And now, this admonition is for you, O priests. If you do not listen, and if you do not set your heart to honour My name, says the Lord Almighty, I will send a curse upon you, and I will curse your blessings."*
>
> Malachi 2:1 ff.

This strange and horrible curse seems to possess some mysterious quality which makes it able to neutralize every blessing one has previously received from God through His grace. It cannot be reversed by any human wisdom or power except by godly repentance through faith in Christ Jesus our Lord. However, if it enters into the house of the unfaithful one, it destroys all that he is and all that he has.

> *"I will curse your blessings. Yes, I have already cursed them, because you have not set your heart to honour Me."*
> Malachi 2:2

Remember that all your blessings (both spiritual and physical) were inherited from Abraham by a simple act of faith in Christ Jesus the Lord, as it says in the Book of Galatians.

> *"Christ redeemed us from the curse of the law by becoming a curse for us, for it is written: Cursed is everyone who is hung on a tree. He redeemed us in order that the blessing given to Abraham might come to the Gentiles through Christ Jesus, so that by faith we might receive the promise of the Spirit."*
> Galatians 3:13 ff.

Yet Abraham, the original recipient of both the promise and the blessings of God (the man of whom God said, "All peoples on earth will be blessed through you" (Genesis 12:3b), paid the tithe faithfully to Melchizedek the King of Salem (Genesis 14:20)). Therefore, we, as believers and spiritual descendants of Abraham, are without excuse when we evade such a holy demand from the Lord who is still saying,

> *"Bring the whole tithe into the storehouse [...]" "A tithe of everything from the land [...] belongs to the Lord; it is holy to the Lord."*
>
> Malachi 3:10

CHAPTER 10

THE FORM OF THE CURSE IN THE SPIRITUAL REALM

The question of what form the curse that enters into the house of the "thief" or the "robber" takes was revealed to the prophet Zechariah many years before our Lord Jesus Christ was born. Now this is what the Prophet saw:

> "I looked again — and there before me was a flying scroll. He asked me, 'What do you see?' I answered, 'I see a flying scroll, thirty feet long and fifteen feet wide.' 'And he said to me, 'This is the curse that is going out over the whole land; for according to what it says on one side, every thief will be banished, and according to what it says on the other, everyone who swears falsely will be banished. The Lord Almighty declares, "I

> *will send it out, and it will enter the house of the thief and the house of him who swears falsely by My name. It will remain in his house and destroy it, both its timbers and its stones."'"*
>
> Zechariah 5:1-4

I wish I could persuade every Christian to be particularly cautious here and not to consider this a fairy tale or to treat it as though it were science-fiction. No matter how difficult it may be to comprehend the scene described here, there is, in the end, only one good choice to make, and that is to *believe*. God is a Spirit and the things of God can only be discerned spiritually. His deeds are supernatural and can only be discerned by spiritual people.

We understand from the Scripture that these things were shown to the prophet and written down for our learning, correction and encouragement. I strongly believe that the above vision, given to the prophet Zechariah, was not meant to scare us but rather, to draw our attention to God's righteous purposes. The Bible says that "God reveals in order to redeem" (cf. Amos 3:7; Daniel 2:28). However, the prerequisite to lasting redemption is **true repentance**. God's objective in the vision He gave to the prophet Zechariah (Zech.5:1-4) was to warn sinners. Thieves are to make a "180 degree" turn from their misdeeds.

I am fully convinced that you would never wish for such an awful visitation upon your own house. I believe with all my heart that, as a Christian, you will never desire such an awful curse to alight on your roof. May God forbid it! Say a loud "Amen" to this!

Instead, may the Lord richly bless your home and supply you bountifully with oil, wine and grain. May the Lord preserve every life in your house and grant you favour. May you never give reason for the curse to come upon your house! The flying scroll is out there in the world, but you don't want it to come anywhere near your dwelling-place. Am I right?

Unlike the Prophet Zechariah, who saw the curse like a flying scroll, King Solomon saw the curse like flying birds. In the Book of Proverbs, King Solomon stated that,

> *"Like a fluttering sparrow or a darting swallow, an undeserved curse does not come to rest."*
>
> Proverbs 26:2

"This is the curse that is going out over the whole land;..."

(cf. Zech. 5:1-4)

The Holy Scriptures declare that

> *"The Lord's curse is on the house of the wicked, but he blesses the home of the righteous."*
>
> Proverbs 3:33

Whether it be like a bird or a scroll, the curse obviously has the ability to fly over, to enter into and to remain in the thief's house until all its timber and stones are destroyed. Let us briefly examine the characteristics of the "flying scroll."

(1) It goes (or flies) out over "the whole land." The Hebrew word for "land" can also mean "earth," and in this instance, I believe the whole world is meant (compare Zechariah 5:1-4 with Proverbs 26:2, where it mentions birds that are certainly not limited to the Promised Land or even to one small area of the world).

(2) Like a satellite, the flying scroll transmits or sends certain afflictions and destructive messages: declarations that cause harm and embarrassment to the unrighteous person, namely "the thief" or "him who swears falsely by My name" (see Zechariah 5:3).

(3) The "flying scroll" is very intelligent. It knows how to sneak into, or manoeuvre itself through the thief's doorway. As described above, it has the ability to enter into (i.e. to penetrate or break into) the home of the robber. There is no sub-human, human or even super-human power able

to undo this curse except the power of God, which is in Jesus Christ.
(4) The "flying scroll" is obedient. It obeys God without question. It never returns to Him until it has accomplished its assigned duty (see Zechariah 5:4).

Duty of the Flying Scroll

The declaration on both sides of the flying scroll is not a judgment against the righteous, but rather against the unrighteous person. It is directed against the "thief," and Scripture calls those men and women who rob God of tithes and offerings that rightly belong to Him, thieves. The curse is intended to destroy the existence, the achievements and the blessings of the liar who swears falsely in God's name in order that he or she may not take God's glory and honour for granted. The punishment inflicted is intended to awaken the unrighteous person's sense of respect for God. The curse:

1. Enters into the house of the wicked (i.e. of the thief and of the one who swears falsely in God's name) to banish them (i.e. to dismiss or drive them out with force). They are dislodged and driven out of their comfortable homes which they have built with God's tithes. Their very existence breaks down due to the afflictions inflicted on them by the crushing effect of the curse.
2. Consumes (i.e. eats up, devours or destroys completely) the entire existence of the liar and

the thief. The flying scroll is what I would call a "divine devourer" since it has a strong consuming and destructive power that has been given to it by God Himself. Instead of having God rebuke "the satanic devourer" who would destroy the fruit of the ground, the evil attitude of the thief prompts the Lord to release more pressure, more affliction and more sorrow on him. The flying scroll comes into the house of the thief only to destroy. Who can rebuke it, and what can dissuade it from taking the course assigned to it? Only repentance, or a one hundred and eighty degree turn to God; only reconciliation with the Lord followed by obedience in the matter of tithes and offerings.

The flying scroll can only listen to God's voice and back off — not to yours. *Your* voice is hearkened to only after you have agreed to submit obediently to the will of God. There is no man who can rebuke a curse merely with his natural strength; it can only be done in total obedience to God through the anointing of His Spirit. That is why the Scripture says,

> *"[...] and we will be ready to punish every act of disobedience, once your obedience is complete."*
> 2. Corinthians 10:6

As the Scripture says, these things were written down for our correction, encouragement and learning.

That is why every thief, most especially those who habitually rob God, should take this very seriously to heart.

God said, if we bring tithes and offerings into His storehouse, He will rebuke the devourer for our sakes. It is God who has the full mandate and the supreme authority to silence the devourer for you and your entire family. He does this on the condition that you obey and bring to Him, what you have been stealing from Him over the past years, namely, His tithes and offerings.

Scripture teaches that as long as you have not fully obeyed, the devourer will continue to prey on your existence until you do. The "satanic devourer" (cf. Mal. 3:11) and "the divine devourer" (cf. Zech. 5:1-4) can both be controlled by God. In fact, they know Him and listen to Him. They also fear and obey Him. The only possible way to obtain a covering or protective shield is to surrender fully to God. What you need to do now is to submit to His will and obey Him. Do not enter into debate with God as to whether tithing is still a valid principle in this New Testament era or not. "Are we still obliged by law to offer sacrifices in the twenty-first century Christian era, or is this just a trick by today's ministers to extort money from church members?" you may ask. You will save yourself time, money, peace and health if you simply obey and do all that God has said in the Holy Scriptures.

Mary, the mother of Jesus once said to the servants at the wedding in Cana of Galilee,

"Do whatever He tells you."
John 2:5

In Matthew 5:18, Jesus said, "I tell you the truth, until heaven and earth disappear, not the smallest letter, not the least stroke of a pen will by any means disappear from the Law until everything is accomplished." Earlier on, in verse 17, He said, *"Do not think that I have come to abolish the Law or the Prophets; I have not come to abolish them but to fulfil them."*

If Jesus had wanted to abolish tithing, He would not have encouraged the scribes and the Pharisees to continue tithing. He said to them,

> *"Woe to you. teachers of the law and Pharisees, you hypocrites! You give a tenth of your spices — mint, dill and cummin. But you have neglected the more important matters of the law — justice, mercy and faithfulness. You should have practised the latter, without neglecting the former."*
> Matthew 23:23

What are the "former" practises? Jesus specifically spoke here concerning the practise of tithing and bringing offerings, a practise which should never be discontinued or neglected. Tithing and offering, Jesus declared, should continue; however, the more important matters of the law — justice, mercy and faithfulness — should be even more strictly upheld.

Justice, i.e. being honest, dealing fairly with one's fellows and desisting from fraud, cheating or any other kind of falsehood, was to be considered more vital than coming into God's presence with goods which had, perhaps, been robbed from the poor to be offered as tithes. It was this temptation to "rob Peter to pay Paul" that the Lord was warning the Scribes and the Pharisees about; in New Testament times, both groups were well-known for their casuistry and trickery.

The Bible says that God hates robbery and iniquity (Isaiah 61:8). But "to do what is right and just is more acceptable to the Lord than sacrifice" (Proverbs 21:3).

Mercy is the exercise of compassion towards the weak, the fatherless, orphans, the stranger, the helpless etc. Mercy was deemed more befitting by Jesus than the tithing of mint, dill and cummin. Jesus challenged his listeners to be more considerate, tender, kind, generous and merciful towards other people rather than to approach God ostentatiously and with a hypocritical attitude. In the Book of Hosea Scripture says,

> "For I desire mercy and not sacrifice [...]"
>
> Hosea 6:6

Jesus was asking the Scribes and the Pharisees to walk in faith. He was challenging them to offer the tithes to God in an attitude of real spiritual worship and not with the supercilious mindset that they had been evidencing until then. He warned them against trying to please onlookers instead of God. Their flamboyant display, designed to impress the people, was severely condemned by the Lord and declared to be an abomination. God is a Spirit, as Scripture says, and whoever comes to Him must do so in Spirit and in truth (John 4:24), that is, in true faith and in the fear of God. An offering made to God in secret and with an upright heart would always be rewarded by the Lord in public. The Scribes and the Pharisees of Jesus' time loved to show off. They displayed their piety openly and were careful to make a "show" of everything they did. (Does that not remind you of some Christian groups today?) They were advised by the Lord to continue doing good deeds, but to do them from inward, heartfelt faith and not merely from a desire to impress human onlookers.

The Satanic And The Divine Devourer

The "flying scroll" consumes and destroys totally. Its consuming power is so fierce and so terrifying that the Scripture says it can even destroy the stones of the houses into which it enters.

The "flying scroll" also has patience. The Bible says,

> *"It will remain in his house [the house of the thief and of him who swears falsely by God's name] and destroy it, both its timbers and its stones."*
> Zechariah 5:4

It remains there until the duty assigned it by God is accomplished. So instead of God rebuking the "satanic devourer" (cf. Mal. 3:11) and telling him to depart from the person's home and life, He sends the flying scroll, the "divine devourer" (cf. Zech. 5:1-4) to add even more afflictions and pain to the thief and the one who swears falsely in God's name – a liar. Side by side, they both perform their work until the thief and the liar are no more! Christians have told me that this sounds quite ridiculous to them; but it is nonetheless true. You can choose either to believe it or to try and "bind" its effects in the name of Jesus. However, you should remember that it was Jesus Himself who said,

> *"I tell you the truth, until heaven and earth disappear, not the smallest letter, not the least stroke of a pen, will by any means disappear from the law until everything is accomplished."*
> Matthew 5:18

Would any true Christian dispute that? Submit to Christ and His word; bring the tithe and generous offerings into God's storehouse now. Test God and see if He does not mean what He said in Malachi 3:10.

Not Called To Be Cursed

Dear reader, you are not appointed or called by God to be cursed. Jesus Christ did not die on the cross for you only to surrender your precious life to the destroyer. It is not God's intention to plague you and your family with various kinds of diseases such as He brought upon the Egyptians. Instead, He has predestined you to eternal, spiritual blessings. God has called you in Christ to bestow on you His eternal glory and blessing. God declares in the Book of Deuteronomy that,

> *"You are a people holy to the Lord your God. The Lord your God has chosen you out of all the peoples on the face of the earth to be His people, His treasured possession."*
>
> Deuteronomy 7:6

From this Scripture, if only you were to be honest to yourself, you would realize that God's heart and mind are full of precious thoughts, plans of peace, good health and abundance of blessings for you and your entire family. You are never one of those common folk walking around town; you are not a half-rusted or broken fragment of a jewel lying on the floor. God chose you by means of a careful and precise process of selection. In fact, in God's treasuries there are found no defiled jewels but only such as are holy and pure, and that is just what you are. You are too special, too precious to be cursed or discarded. No curse can rest on you. Why not? Because you are holy. The Lord declares by His word that you are "holy" and "special" to Him; and if this is true, how could He turn round and curse you? However, what the Lord is asking of you is total submission and obedience to His word. Since mercy, favour and blessings are the reward for obedience, the Lord promises to show you mercy and to bless you as you walk obediently with Him.

> *"If you pay attention to these laws and are careful to follow them, then the Lord your God will keep His covenant of love with you, as He swore to your forefathers. He will love you and bless you and increase your numbers. He will bless the fruit of your womb, the crops of your land — your grain, new wine and oil — the calves of your herds and the lambs of your flocks in the land which He swore to your forefathers to give you. You will be blessed more than any other people; none of your men or women will be childless, nor any of your livestock without young."*
>
> Deuteronomy 7:12 ff.

CHAPTER 11

TAKING THE BLESSING BY FAITH

The Scripture says,

> *"The Lord's curse is on the house of the wicked."*
>
> Proverbs 3:33a

However, as a Christian you are not "wicked". You have not stolen from God something that He considers "holy" (i. e. the tithe), and since your hands are clean, and your conscience clear, the Lord's curse will not come upon your house. Rather, the Bible says: *"He blesses the home of the righteous"* (Proverbs 3:33b).

It is not your portion to be cursed but to be blessed! Your blessings were pre-planned, pre-determined, pre-destined and pre-ordained in the past for your present and future. All you need to do is to obey the voice of the Lord your God. You will not receive blessings by arguing. You will not prevail by debating and complaining when it comes to obeying the voice of the Lord.

Do not hurry to make a list of the good things you have done as a Christian. God knows them all. Your numerous activities, good works and sacrifices are certainly all good. Yet the Bible says,

"To obey is better than sacrifice."
1. Samuel 15:22a

Obedience to God's word, to His ordinances and commandments, brings forth a good deal of fruit and many good results. In the book of Deuteronomy, chapter 28, God promises to make His blessings "accompany" you. You will not be able to move faster than these blessings, I assure you, no matter how you travel! They are blessings which are able to sustain you during your whole life on earth, and afterwards they will be passed on to your children's children, even to a thousand generations because of your love for and obedience to *"the Lord your God" (Deuteronomy 28:1 ff.).*

If you believe in blessings, then please pause here and open your Bible to the twenty-eighth chapter of the Book of Deuteronomy and read from verses three to fourteen. The rest of the chapter, i.e. from verse sixteen to verse sixty-eight, should be left for the wicked and the liar to peruse.

The Lord Jesus Christ, our High Priest, raised up according to the order of King Melchizedek, has set us free from the curse of the law. We are therefore no longer being guided by the law but by grace through faith in Christ Jesus.

Jesus Christ has given us victory over the curse of the law having Himself become a curse for our sake on the cross of Calvary, in order that we, having believed, might inherit the pre-planned, pre-ordained, pre-determined and pre-destined blessing promised to our spiritual father Abraham.

> *"Christ redeemed us from the curse of the law by becoming a curse for us, for it is written: "Cursed is everyone who is hung on a tree." He redeemed us in order that the blessing given to Abraham might come to the Gentiles through Christ Jesus, so that by faith we might receive the promise of the Spirit."*
> Galatians 3:13 ff.

The apostle Paul greatly rejoiced in this victory which we have in Christ over the curse of the law. That is why he said,

> *"Thanks be to God! He gives us the victory through our Lord Jesus Christ."*
> 1. Corinthians 15:57

This victory triumphs over the curse, all manner of diseases and all satanic powers through the atoning Blood of our Lord Jesus Christ.

The Bible reveals the great love with which God loved us (John 3:16) and that even when we were yet sinners - fornicators, liars, adulterers and adulteresses, armed robbers, deceivers, witches, wizards, occultists, palm-readers, fortune-tellers etc. - He sent His beloved Son Jesus Christ down to earth to die for us. There is every reason for us to rejoice in that.

Having been forgiven all our sins, delivered from various bondages and healed of all manner of diseases, we as believers must learn to love the Lord with all our strength, mind, heart and substance. We must seek to express our sincere gratitude and thankfulness to the Lord as we persevere in obeying His ordinance concerning tithes and offerings.

Abraham's Challenging Faith

We do not have to wait till we receive a personal revelation concerning "tithing to God" before we reach out to obey the Lord. What is written in the Book is sufficient to elicit our obedience. The tithe is said to be "holy" to the Lord. There is no point in hoping or waiting for God to change His mind concerning that!

Abraham, the progenitor of the Jews and the founder of the Hebrew race, lived before both the prophet

Moses and the law. If, without the law, Abraham offered tithes to the high priest of Salem, King Melchizedek, what hinders us from giving equally generously to that most excellent King and High Priest of our Confession, the One who loved us and gave His life as a ransom for our redemption?

Abraham had not been saved by Melchizedek's blood, nor had he been delivered from lying, compromise and fear by any action of the King of Salem; but the Lord Jesus has done that for us all. He has forgiven all our sins, raised us from spiritual death and reconciled us to God the Father. Jesus has healed all our diseases and blessed us to overflowing with new covenant blessings: eternal life, heavenly dwellings, peace with God, perpetual spiritual riches, everlasting joy and hope for the future.

If Abraham could offer the tithe to Melchizedek, who blessed him on the way home from the battlefield (Genesis 14:18 ff.), how much less should we as New Testament Christians, a people dearly loved by God, neglect any opportunity to offer to God those things which He has deemed to be holy, namely, tithes and offerings?

Abraham loved God, but he also respected the person of King Melchizedek. He gave him the tithe freely and from his heart. Abraham was neither commanded nor requested to give the tithe to Melchizedek; the high priest never asked for it. Everything was done reciprocally out of deep and sincere mutual love. Abraham simply believed and loved God, and therefore He offered the tithe to King Melchizedek, who was at that time the earthly representative of God, the Most High.

Many of the arguments, debates, discussions and complaints we indulge in concerning tithing in today's churches are manifestly due to a lack of love, divine insight and perception of what the Lord Jesus has accomplished for us. Scripture commands us to praise the Lord for His acts of power (Psalm 150:2). We seem to know the truth, but when it comes to the "acts of the believers" we always miss it. We say a lot but do little. "Saying" is one thing but "doing" is another. The Bible says we are to be "doers and not hearers only". We are called to go ahead and perform through faith acts of justice and mercy and everything that pleases God (Hebrews 11:6; Matthew 23:23). Bringing tithes and offerings to God in this era of faith can only be done in a perfect manner of confidential trust in the Lord and not by command or law.

Tithing In Spirit And In Truth

During this last period of the dispensation of grace, God is seeking for people who will approach Him:
1) By faith (Hebrew 11:6);
2) In spirit (i.e. with their hearts (John 4:23-24)); and
3) In truth (John 4:23-24).

The Bible says it is with the heart (or spirit) we believe and are justified (Romans 10:9 ff.). Our righteousness is perfected by exercising our faith in authentic, practical works such as tithing. Hence, tithes and offerings brought in faith to God will never fail to attract God's favour on the giver. Offerings made in truth always set the giver free; he or she is freed (liberated) from doubt, fear and poverty.

We offer the tithes and offerings to God and not to men or organizations, whoever they may be. And we do it not because we have been commanded to do so, but because we have been granted a perfect understanding of who the Lord Jesus is — the High Priest of our Confession in heaven — and of what this Jesus has done for us: He has forgiven us our sins and reconciled us to God through His sacrificial death on the cross; He has obtained eternal life for us through faith in His name; He has delivered us from everything that would destroy us and has healed all our diseases and much more. We are witnesses of His goodness and mercy.

In Hebrews we read,

> "We do not have a high priest who is unable to sympathise with our weaknesses."
> Hebrews 4:15

He understands your situation perfectly. The financial burden you are now facing is clear to Him.

Jesus has not condemned you, but the devil has. However, in all these things, the Lord has carried you on eagles' wings over many troubles until now. If you look back a few years or months ago and remember the hardships and the attacks, the pains and the distress that nearly engulfed you and your entire family, the financial burden that almost overwhelmed you, and almost made you give up, and if you remember how God supernaturally held your hand and led you through it all, you will pause in your reading here and give heartfelt thanks to the Lord Jesus for the things He has done for you and your family. How ungrateful is that man or woman in whose heart and mouth there is no room for the words "thank you"! Why are so many of today's believers inflicted with ingratitude? One reason is that they lack the fear of God; another is that they have deliberately purposed in their hearts to avoid doing the works by which they should be expressing their faith. All the unnecessary debates and arguments in today's churches are the result of this. Refusing to "think" leads to a lack of "thanks". A short memory is one of the great causes of ingratitude in the house of God. Gratitude is said to be a law of nature. Your gratitude to the Lord will determine your attitude in this life which yields later to an attitude of eternal abundance.

The Scripture declares that as you go on obeying what the Lord has commanded you, He will set you high above all nations on earth (Deuteronomy 28:1). As you diligently continue to obey and to do His will, He promises to *"make you the head, not the tail; [...] you will always be at the top, never at the bottom" (Deuteronomy 28:13).*

CHAPTER 12

IN TITHES AND OFFERINGS

God said to the believers of old, "Yet you rob me!" But they answered Him rebelliously and disrespectfully, *"How do we rob you?" (Malachi 3:8).*

The Lord answered, *"In tithes and offerings"* *(Malachi 3:8).*

Although the Lord patiently replied to their sheepish question, many among us today are still stumbling over the same truth. The Lord said to them, "In tithes and offerings". Are we still going to keep asking Him the same question over and over again?

Are you still fondly attached to your worldly conviction that tithing is a thing of the past? How long are you going to insult God by insisting against all the evidence from His Word that His ministers should leave out what you term the "blinding shadow" or the "Old Testament stuff"? Do you really feel more spiritual refraining from tithing? Is the Christ you claim to serve embarrassed when you tithe? Do you sincerely feel that giving tithes to God does nothing other than to nullify the finished work of Christ on the cross? Perhaps you have other probing questions to ask. However, it is my great privilege to inform you that, although many of the streets, buildings and other aspects of the infrastructure in your community or country may have undergone drastic change, the Lord God of Abraham, Isaac and Jacob, the same God Moses, David and Jesus of Nazareth worshipped, has undergone no change whatsoever! The Bible says,

> *"He is the same yesterday, today, and forever."*
>
> Hebrews 13:8

Will God Almighty change because you are not convinced of His Word? Judge for yourself. If the practise of tithing is obsolete in this New Testament dispensation, then you might just as well dispense with all the blessings we are meant to inherit from our father Abraham.

In spite of already having the promise of Divine blessings, Abraham made sure that he also obtained the blessing of Melchizedek, the king of Salem and high priest of God Most High. The Scripture says that Abraham gave Melchizedek a tenth of all the spoil from the battle (Genesis 14:18 ff.). If Abraham's faith in God (and Abraham was the man in whom "all peoples on earth" were to be blessed) (Genesis 12:3) combined with his habit of tithing led to such blessing, how on earth do we manage to convince ourselves that in the New Testament era tithing is wrong?

In James 2:14 the apostle asks,

> *"What good is it, my brothers, if a man claims to have faith but has no deeds?"*

And the conclusion that he draws is,

> *"Faith without deeds is dead."*
> James 2:20

In his endeavour to maintain an active faith Abraham added deeds to his faith by offering a tenth of all he had gained to the high priest of God Most High.

Faith that is dead merely argues. It challenges and questions sensible, scriptural and spiritual counsel. Faith that is dead is not only dead for itself, but it also seeks to impose death on all around it. If you have become a victim of some form of dead faith, just pause here in your reading and pray that your own faith may be immediately resurrected from the dead!

In the Book of James we read,

> *"Was not our ancestor Abraham considered righteous for what he did*

> *when he offered his son Isaac on the altar?"*
>
> James 2:21 ff.

Abraham gave the tithe, and he was willing to sacrifice Isaac. What have you given to the Kingdom of God? What sacrifices have you been prepared to make?

The flying scroll curse has alighted on many roofs and in many homes. It is causing great havoc, ruining many homes, families, marriages, businesses and projects, and shattering many dreams. And all because of manifest disobedience to the Word of God!

You may consider tithing to be an issue that has to do only with antiquity, but the curse that necessarily accompanies disobedience cannot be denied. For there is no such thing as a contemporary curse or an archaic curse. A curse remains a curse, and it is never too old to destroy and never too new to cause grievous loss. A curse is always a curse and must be dealt with immediately. How? Through the only name under heaven given to men by which we must be saved, the name of Jesus Christ (Acts 4:12).

There is no human or scientific mechanism by which a curse can be obliterated. A detergent that could be used to wash off the curse from the sinner's roof has not yet been invented or discovered. Attempting to abolish a curse by any super-human power other than the wisdom and the power of God which is in Jesus Christ will always prove futile and hopeless. Genuine faith in Jesus Christ is the only key to rebuking and neutralizing the power of the flying-scroll curse (Zechariah 5:1-4).

In Galatians chapter three, we read,

> *"Christ has redeemed us from the curse of the law, having become a curse for us."*
> Galatians 3:13 ff.

Do you understand that? The Bible says you have been redeemed (i.e. bought back, purchased, rescued) from the penalty of the flying-scroll curse that enters the home of the thief and the perjurer to consume it. The Lord Jesus, by His death, has abolished every kind of curse for your sake. The Bible says,

> *"When you were dead in your sins and in the uncircumcision of your sinful nature, God made you alive with Christ. He forgave us all our sins, having cancelled the written code, with its regulations, that was against us and that stood opposed to us; he took it away, nailing it to the cross."*
> Colossians 2:13 ff.

"Like a fluttering sparrow or a darting swallow, an undeserved CURSE does not come to rest." Prov. 26:2

And again, the Bible says,

> *"If the Son sets you free, you will be free indeed."*
>
> John 8:36

In Genesis 14:18-20 there is not one indication that Abraham was helped by Melchizedek, the King of Salem, in his battle against his enemies. There is no statement describing this king as having come out to the battlefield to rescue Abraham from being cut down by a slashing sword. Melchizedek, who was also the high priest of God Most High, did not show up at the battlefield but instead went out *after* the slaughter to meet Abraham with bread and wine in order to refresh him. It was only after Abraham and his servants had completed their warfare that Melchizedek, the King of Salem, met him and blessed him. But regardless of this, Abraham gave him a tenth of all the booty he had obtained during the battle.

Abraham's attitude towards the high priest of Salem should be a challenging and eye-opening example for the New Testament Christian. If we desire Abraham's blessing, then we should learn from his old-fashioned, generous way of expressing his faith. Abraham demonstrated that his faith was not dead by doing. And what he did was to tithe.

Irreverent questions as to whether it is still advisable or needful to tithe in our day and age are simply symptoms of lack of knowledge of the word of God. Those who question the principle of tithing and conduct noisy debates about it are mistaken. They are in error and stumble at the truth because they fail to differentiate between the fulfilment of prophetic Scripture and practical scriptural instruction which continues from the shadow into the light and from law over to faith. Those born under the law were justified by the law. But we are justified by faith through grace in Jesus. However, even in the days of the patriarchs, long before the Law of Moses, the man Abraham operated by faith and was for this reason considered by God as a righteous man and a friend (James 2:23).

If Abraham was able to respond to the high priest Melchizedek by tithing, we as New Testament Christians should be able to do far better for our Lord and Saviour Jesus Christ. After all, Melchizedek did not die for Abraham but the Lord Jesus Christ died for us. Just as Abraham was not forced to offer tithes to Melchizedek, even so we also should voluntarily, lavishly and generously offer our gifts to the Lord without murmuring.

A child of God must act in faith from a sincere and willing heart, in mercy and with justice, by bringing into the storehouse all that by right belongs to God.

CHAPTER 13

THE GENEROSITY OF THE EARLY CHURCH

The brethren in the early church were not required or requested by law or command to bring the tithe into God's storehouse. There was no mention of "a tenth of one's income" among them at all. Instead, they sold their possessions voluntarily and brought the entire proceeds to the apostles to be shared among them; as many as had needs were blessed by their corporate generosity. Their "one hundred percent tithing" habit helped to overcome lack and poverty in their midst. Brothers and sisters who were less well-off were richly comforted by the perfect giving of the others (see Acts 2:44; 4:32, 34).

Those early Christians gave more than just "a tenth" to God. They offered their all (i.e. their one hundred percent love and faith) to God. Even Ananias and Sapphira who we usually sniff at because of their deceit are described as having brought more than a tenth to the apostles. The Bible says they sold their land and kept back *some* of the money. It is likely that perhaps they kept half (50%) of the proceeds or a little less than a half of the total sum involved. But in every sense, I find Ananias and his wife Sapphira to have gone well beyond the tenth of their income that some of today's Christians find so challenging. If, however, they were still considered as "lying to the Holy Spirit" and as worthy of death after donating a goodly fraction of the proceeds of what they had sold, what can we say about those of us who rob God of the tenth and yet still ask Him, "How do we rob You?"

A twenty-first century believer who finds it a struggle to offer the tithe because of doubt, uncertainty or fear is, it would seem to me, simply still learning the ropes of the Christian faith and will, with time, learn to appropriate the Word of God for his or her personal situation so as to overcome all misgivings.

But a deliberate refusal to give tithes and offerings based on a conviction that tithing is merely a remnant of legalistic, Old Testament teaching is a serious error and flies in the face of all biblical evidence. Believers who refuse to tithe are simply destitute of the truth. Such "believers" are plainly described in Scripture as "thieves" or "robbers" irrespective of all their arguments and reasoning. An exception can only be made if someone can truthfully testify that God has not blessed him or her materially at all.

Waiting and hoping for a special revelation before bringing the tithe into God's storehouse puts a Christian beneath the level of Ananias and Sapphira. Ananias and Sapphira would probably have found it easier to give the tenth than to bring the entire sum to God. It was beyond their strength to give all they had to the church. But perhaps bringing a mere tenth of the whole sum could have been more tolerable for them.

If Ananias and his wife were alive and members of our churches today, they would be the best friends of our contemporary ministers, perhaps they would even be considered as prime leadership material. Imagine having a brother and a sister in your church who often bring half of their earned income into God's storehouse. Would they not cause you to rejoice and to give them special VIP treatment? Just picture it! To certain avaricious folk, Ananias and Sapphira would have been something akin to "the patron saints of the church". They would be the centre of attention, being held up as models for the church to follow, especially the "non-tithers". And yet, for all that, Ananias and Sapphira with their ostentatious offering of over ten percent, fell dead at the feet of the apostle Peter because of their lies and their unfaithfulness. May God keep Christians today from such sins!

We often speak disdainfully of such people. And yet I am absolutely sure that Jesus would prefer Ananias and his wife Sapphira to many "believers" of this present generation. During His earthly ministry, the Lord Jesus had to chide the people of Korazin, Bethsaida and Capernaum for their negligence with regard to works of faith.

Their unresponsiveness and their sheer unbelief compelled Jesus to compare them to ungodly cities of old such as Sodom, Tyre and Sidon.

Although the iniquities of Sodom were grievous in the eyes of the Lord Jesus, after having observed and experienced an even worse attitude among the very people He had come to save, He passed the following judicial sentence upon them:

> "*Then Jesus began to denounce the cities in which most of His miracles had been performed, because they did not repent. "Woe to you, Korazin! Woe to you, Bethsaida! If the miracles that were performed in you had been performed in Tyre and Sidon, they would have repented long ago in sackcloth and ashes. But I tell you, it will be more bearable for Tyre and Sidon on the day of judgment than for you. And you, Capernaum, will you be lifted up to the skies? No, you will go down to the depths. If the miracles that were performed in you had been performed in Sodom, it would have remained to this day."*
>
> Matthew 11:20-23

Having been given the very best opportunity to believe, Korazin, Bethsaida and Capernaum were expected to demonstrate faith and to act more zealously than the people of Sodom, Tyre and Sidon, who were overthrown or annihilated because of their sins.

In spite of having heard, seen and experienced magnificent demonstrations of divine power, Korazin, Bethsaida and Capernaum rejected the Lord Jesus and apparently also neglected the less weighty duties of faith.

Their disobedience and unbelief astonished the Lord Jesus so immensely that He pointed out to them their future position and destiny on the day of judgment. Jesus revealed to Korazin, Bethsaida and Capernaum the degree and the heinousness of their wickedness and summarized what he had to say in these words:

> *"But I tell you that it will be more bearable for the Sodom on the day of judgment than for you."*
> Matthew 11:24

I believe the Lord Jesus would have greater compassion on and be more tolerant towards Ananias and Sapphira than towards many Christians of this present century. Many of today's "believers" are more unkind and more ungrateful, unhelpful, rapacious, stingy and avaricious than any of the early Christians. Instead of encouraging, they betray and discourage one another;

instead of caring for the weak and the needy, they despise and neglect them.

The believers in the first century church were united in purpose. They were very "close" and "intimate" in faith, in love, in hope and in the sharing of their material possessions. They sold their property and brought in all the proceeds of the transaction to the feet of the apostles (except Ananias and Saphira who "embezzled" their own funds).

How many honest brethren do we have in our churches today that would be ready to offer all they possess in order to have God's purposes taken care of? "Times have changed," they say. "Things are now very hard," some reiterate. But has God changed concerning His word? If He blessed Abraham, will He not also bless us? If great grace and power rested upon the early church because of their generosity, faith and unity in the Spirit, will we not have more grace and power if we embrace the truth concerning tithing and the basic principles of giving?

The early church was able without doubt to fulfill the golden law. They loved the Lord God with all their heart and also with all their substance. They loved their neighbours as themselves, and they cared for the needy among them. They sold their property and brought the entire proceeds to the house of God. They were a special brand of believers who truly understood the meaning of the word "all". They offered their all to the Almighty.

They recognized God as their absolute source of supply. The term "tithe" was inadequate for them. In fact, it was not included in their vocabulary. Instead, they spoke and practised the language of "all" and not "some". "All" was the language Ananias and Sapphira failed to understand. They hated the language of "all" and embraced the language of "some" and that was why they could not bring all but only some of the proceeds of what they had sold to the apostles.

If you cannot bring all your possessions to God, namely your cars, houses, shares and capital investments, your gold bars, etc., why can you not at least be honest with all the tithe and offering which belong to God?

Presenting only a part (or "some") of the tithe makes you more liable to judgment than even Ananias and Sapphira were. Be frank with yourself and faithful to God. The Scripture says,

> *"God cannot be mocked. A man reaps what he sows."*
>
> Galatians 6:7

CHAPTER 14

HINDRANCES TO TITHING

The Reforms of Nehemiah

Some believers are willing to bring the tithe honestly into the Lord's storehouse, but they nevertheless refrain from doing so because of a lack of justice and order. An unpleasant situation of this kind came to light during the reforms of Nehemiah when the rulers of the house of God neglected their assigned duties in order to take care of their personal interests. Nehemiah introduced his reformation because he wanted to establish order and to bring back discipline to the house of God.

Because of lack of food in God's storehouse (the temple), the Levites who were chosen to minister to God in His Sanctuary left their spiritual duties to work in the fields. They resigned from being ministers of God and resorted to agricultural pursuits until Nehemiah came on the scene to restore order to the temple and to re-establish worship in its appropriate place in the Lord's sanctuary. Nehemiah contended with the cruel rulers over the house of Israel, who had probably misused the funds donated by the people, and helped to create an atmosphere which paved the way for the proper worship of God.

Nehemiah was able to encourage the Levites to come back and occupy their spiritual positions and to resume their service in the temple. He succeeded in motivating the people of God to bring the tithes and offerings to support kingdom work.

When justice and equity had prevailed in the land, the Bible records that the people of God felt free to give abundantly to the house of God.

> *"I also learned that the portions assigned to the Levites had not been given to them, and that all the Levites and singers responsible for the service had gone back to their own fields. So I rebuked the officials and asked them, 'Why is the house of God neglected?' Then I called them together and stationed them at their posts. All Judah brought the tithes of grain, new wine and oil into the storerooms."*
>
> Nehemiah 13:10 ff.

The Reforms of Hezekiah

A tragic phenomenon which was witnessed by King Hezekiah during his reign compelled him to introduce a rapid reformation in Israel. He commanded the people of God to give back to the priests and the Levites the portion which belonged to them.

The Scripture declares:

> *"He [Hezekiah] ordered the people living in Jerusalem to give the portion due to the priests and Levites so that they could devote themselves to the Law of the Lord. As soon as the order went out, the Israelites generously gave the firstfruits of their grain, new wine, oil and honey and all that the fields produced. They brought a great amount, a tithe of everything. [...] And Azariah the chief priest, from the family of Zadok, answered, 'Since the people began to bring their contributions to the temple of the Lord, we have had enough to eat and plenty to spare, because the Lord has blessed His people, and this great amount is left over."*
> 2. Chronicles 31:4-5,10

We can see from these Scriptures that the reforms of both Nehemiah and Hezekiah brought great change and order to the house of God, thus enabling God's people to give generously, obediently and faithfully towards God's work.

We can also not avoid the implication that the damage done to God's house and his cause was the result of improper administration by the rulers of His house (comparable to pastors, elders, etc. today). God is here warning leaders, and especially those who are responsible for tithe-collecting, to refrain from anything that even remotely resembles exploitation, cheating or manipulation.

Such behaviour on the part of ministers often leads the people of God into doubt, uncertainty, fear and confusion, and this later affects and breaks their attitude concerning giving freely to God the things that rightfully belong to Him.

God's retributive judgment therefore dawns on such transgressors, as is clearly illustrated within the pages of the Holy Scriptures;

> *"So I will come near to you for judgment. I will be quick to testify against sorcerers, adulterers and perjurers, against those who defraud labourers of their wages, who oppress the widows and the fatherless."*
> Malachi 3:5

> *"The Sovereign Lord has sworn by His holiness: 'The time will surely come when you will be taken away with hooks, the last of you with fish-hooks. You will each*

> *go straight out through breaks in the wall [...] Bring your sacrifices every morning, **your** tithes every three years [...] Brag about your freewill offerings – boast about them, you Israelites, for this is what you love to do,' declares the Sovereign Lord."*
>
> Amos 4:2-5

> *"And now, this admonition is for you, O priests [who exploit the people of God]. If you do not listen, and if you do not set your heart to honour My name, says the Lord Almighty, I will send a curse upon you, and I will curse your blessings."*
>
> Malachi 2:1 ff.

It is a great privilege to be called by God to minister to His people. It is honourable to be referred to as the "pastor" (or "shepherd") over the Lord's flock. It is wonderful to walk through your congregation with all eyes fixed on you as the "man in the mirror". The feel of trust, love and respect a pastor or minister of God receives from the congregation is so amazing that there is no adequate word to describe it. However, as a leader, entrusted with the Lord's flock, God requires from you absolute honesty and faithfulness. Taking advantage of the people's love, respect and submissiveness to manipulate their innocence is something that God can and will not ignore or take lightly. That is why we have the Lord's stern warning to all leaders who practise shady financial dealings, manipulation and extortion.

Should Pastors Also Pay Tithes?

Pastors who are personally faithful in tithing to God are also often found to be honest and true to their congregation. The Bible records that the Levites (the ministers of God) were also commanded to bring the tenth of all the tithes of Israel which they received into the storehouse of God.

The Bible declares that,

"The Levites are to bring a tenth of the tithes up to the house of our God, to the storerooms of the treasury."
Nehemiah 10:38

A Levite or a minister of God, who receives wages but does not recognize the importance of tithing his income endangers himself and lays his life bare as a prey to the predator (the devourer). In his wilful ignorance, he sticks his chest out in pride, only to be struck down by the anger of the Lord.

The Bible reveals that avaricious, self-serving leaders may eventually lose their lives if they continue to be "wise in their own eyes" by neglecting and despising the holy things of God.

> *"The LORD said to Moses, 'Speak to the Levites [the ministers of God] and say to them: "When you receive from the Israelites the tithe I give you for your inheritance, you must present a tenth of that tithe as the Lord's offering. [...] By presenting the best part of it, you will not be guilty in this matter; then you will not defile the holy offerings of the Israelites, and you will not die."'"*
>
> Numbers 18:25-26,32

God is no respecter of persons. The Scripture declares that whoever fears Him and does righteously, God will accept him (Acts 10:34 ff.). As the ministers of God offer the tithe out of the gifts or the income received from the church, the gifts, the tithes and the offerings of the entire congregation are simultaneously sanctified before the Lord.

> *"Then you [the Levites or spiritual leaders] will not defile the holy offerings of the Israelites, and you will not die."*
>
> Numbers 18:32b

The tithe is holy, absolutely holy to the Lord and must be handled and treated with reverential fear.

We are therefore safe to conclude that the gifts, offerings and tithes of the congregation are made acceptable to the required standard of God through the scrupulous tithing of His ministers.

Counsel to Covenant-Partners

Despite all the hindrances you may encounter with regard to tithing, it is strictly advisable to take heed to what God has declared to the churches. In Deuteronomy 12:5-6 (read the whole passage) God's word assists us greatly in avoiding any practises that could result in a curse. The Word of God teaches us to prayerfully seek the place where He chooses to put His name, and offer the tithes and offerings there.

Generations of Disobedience

Some believers are bound by generations of disobedience which stretch back to the days of their miserly and disobedient ancestors who not only disobeyed the ordinances and the commandments of God, but have also hindered their descendants from coming to the knowledge of the truth.

> *"I the Lord do not change. So you, O descendants of Jacob, are not destroyed. Ever since the time of your forefathers you have turned away from My decrees and have not kept them. Return to Me, and I will return to you, says the Lord Almighty. But you ask, 'How are we to*

> *return?' [...] 'In tithes and offerings,' says the Lord."*
>
> Malachi 3:6 ff.

Although they seem to love God, these believers find it very difficult to honour the Lord with their material substance. No matter what teaching they receive, they consider their physical needs and desires to be much more important than giving forth their substance to be used by men who claim to be God's servants. Their miserliness involves doubts, mistrust, uncertainty, ignorance, fear and simple disobedience. However, you can deliver yourself from such bondage if you want to. Make a decision to obey God now and be determined to keep it. Stand the challenge of testing Malachi 3:10 and find out if God will not honour His infallible Word.

The fathers departed from the Lord with regard to both the tithes and their offerings. They blindly disobeyed the Lord's ordinance of tithing and thus prevented their children from receiving the Lord's blessing in their lives.

However, now that the truth about the result of the fathers' disobedience has come to light, I can only recommend that the children wake up and accept the challenge to obey God now. It is time for the children to return to God in the matter of tithes and offerings and do what the LORD requires. The Bible tells us that obedience is better than sacrifice (1. Samuel 15:22) and that the reward for obedience is favour and blessing (Deuteronomy 28:1 ff.).

If parents sin against the Lord by disobeying His commandments, the curse which results from disobedience passes on from them to their children, even to the fourth generation (Numbers 14:18). However, if the parents obey, the blessing on their lives overtakes them and moves ahead into future generations.

When children are taught how to give to God, the Bible says that when they grow up into adulthood, they will never depart from what they have learnt (Proverbs 22:6).

Generous parents will always have their children imitating them in their manner of giving to God and to their fellow-men.

Return to God, then He will also return to you. He has shown you the way to do this in Malachi 3:6-8: "In tithes and offerings." A family or household which chooses to obey God "in tithes and offerings" will be walking in the path of obedience and blessing and will know something of the protection and sustenance of the Lord.

Tithe today and you will put God in a position to bind the devourer *tight* for your sake.

Remember that disobedience attracts a curse (Malachi 2:1 ff.; Deuteronomy 28:15) and that it is the curse that makes men poor (Deuteronomy 28:20; 1. Samuel 2:7). Poverty forces men to steal (Proverbs 30:7

ff.), and whoever steals profanes the name of the Lord (Exodus 20:15; 20:7; Proverbs 30:9). And those who steal and profane God's name will never inherit the kingdom of God (Exodus 20:15; 1. Corinthians 6:9 ff.).

CHAPTER 15

IMPORTANT FACTORS INVOLVED IN TRUE TITHING

True tithing involves the following vital factors:

(1) FAITH

By faith, the believer (or God's covenant partner) understands that *a tenth* of his income is a sacred portion which belongs solely to the Lord (Lev.27:30) and as such, must be treated with absolute reverence.

By faith, the believer hopes and trusts God for the promised "windows of heaven" to be opened, for his barns to be filled with the abundance of the blessings of heaven, and for the mouth of the devourer to be rebuked and firmly shut in Jesus name.

Faith expressed through tithing brings great pleasure to God because it recognizes God's presence and His ability to provide every need. Hence it is impossible for the believer to please God without faith, the Scriptures say (Hebrews 11:1,6).

Faith is a fact, but faith is also an act. Acting upon God's word through faith, has the potential to bring forth powerful results. Giving to God in total submission to His word is an act of faith which involves us taking the blessing promised in the past for our future and letting it be made manifest in the present. Therefore also Christ said, *"Have faith in God," (Mark 11:22).*

(2) GOOD CONSCIENCE

A good conscience is of great value when we bring the tithes and other offerings into God's house because those who collect the tithes and offerings, the New Testament equivalents of the Levites and priests, are mere human beings. A tithe-giver needs to realize that, obediently bringing this offering in agreement with the commandment of God, requires an act of faith and a well disciplined *conscience.* This would enable the tithe-giver to avoid the temptation of being lured into criticism concerning the humanness of the clergies whom God has appointed to collect and utilize the tithe (or the money) he is giving.

Tithe-givers should not burden themselves with care about how the tithes are being utilized by those appointed for this purpose in the church. Instead, it must be noticed that when we "give" by faith, we give to God and not to men. The believer must simply *trust* and maintain *a good conscience* when it comes to giving for instance, the tithe or offering to the Lord. Although the *visible* recipients, *(i.e. the clergy, priest, pastor, bishop etc.)* are *men* yet, it must be understood that the ***original*** or ***initial* recipient** of such holy *things, (such as the tithes* and *offerings)* is the Lord Himself. Your motive for offering the tithe and other gifts, must be directed to the honour and to the glorification of the Lord, as it is written:

> *"Whatever you do,* ***do it all for the glory of God.****"*
>
> 1. Corinthians 10:31b

It is therefore imperative to have faith, holding your conscience stable and pure in the fear of the Lord.

> *"Holding on to faith and a good conscience. Some have rejected these and have shipwrecked their faith."*
>
> 1. Timothy 1:19

Doubt and a bad conscience are the two great deadly enemies of faith. They are hindrances to growth and progress and endanger believers at every step. God commands us to bring the tenth of all our income into His storehouse without doubt. The malpractice or the ill manners of a church elder or leader whose job it is to collect or administer the tithes should never deter you from obeying the Lord. Just believe that God is able to deal with any rogue and to punish any blackguard. Never forget this: vengeance belongs to the Lord alone and not to you. God requires from His stewards that they are faithful in all His house, and when such men are unfaithful or dishonest, God has His way of dealing with them (cf. Deuteronomy 32:35; Malachi 2:1 ff.; Numbers 18:32).

Every believer is obliged to receive this revelation with a good and clear conscience, namely that the tithe of his or her income is not man's property but the Lord's; it is property "set aside" for the Lord (cf. Leviticus 27:30).

(3) JUSTICE

With justice, one avoids cheating, lying and stealing the things which God has ordained as holy for Himself. Through the spirit of justice, the tithe-giver is careful to avoid any false balance in God's presence (Proverbs 11:1). Thus, he offers completely to God the things that are God's. Unlike Ananias and Sapphira, who lied to the Holy Spirit concerning their giving and who also received an instant judgment from the Lord Acts 5:1-11), the covenant partner should endeavour to exhibit a high moral standard of spiritual understanding and discipline, especially concerning those things which are regarded as being in the perfect will of God (Luke 20:25). Equity and an equal balance should be the order of the day for every Christian who fears God.

(4) MERCY

In Luke 6:36 we read, "Be merciful, just as your Father is merciful". A heart full of mercy reveals the nature of God to all men, even to the ungrateful. A believer who is merciful and kind is always willing to please his Maker and to fulfil all His desires on earth.

A church full of merciful Christians and scrupulously honest leaders will always grow and increase amazingly. Why? Because its members are spiritually fed and well nourished by God's servants. Such leaders will be well taken care of by their merciful and generous church members who ensure by giving that there is always enough "food" in God's house.

> *"Woe to you, teachers of the law and Pharisees, you hypocrites! You give a tenth of your spices – mint, dill and cummin. But you have neglected the more important matters of the law – justice, mercy and faithfulness. You should have practised the latter, without neglecting the former."*
>
> Matthew 23:23

From this scripture, we can easily recognize the hot displeasure of Christ as He rebuked and condemned the Scribes and the Pharisees for their crafty acts and their hypocrisy. For they paid the tithe for all to see, but neglected those vital, precious attributes of justice, mercy and faith, which are imperative and much more preferable in the sight of the Living God.

(5) FEAR

Fear in this case means reverence. In all things and in all ways, God demands genuine, reverential fear from His people. The people of God should reverence and honour Him no matter how they feel or where they are. All those who come into His presence should recognize and behold Him with awesome respect and deep praise. Without the fear of the Lord, no one in heaven, on earth or under the earth can claim to have received any perfect knowledge and understanding of the sovereign Spirit.

Bringing tithes to this invisible God with the strong confidence that He *is,* reveals reverential fear for Him in the heart of the believer. However, the disobedient or stiff-necked Christian who care less about honouring the Lord or paying any homage to His glorious Name, the Lord threatens with a curse (cf. Malachi 2:1 ff.).

A man who fears God truly knows God.

> *"Be sure to set aside a tenth of all that your fields produce each year. Eat the tithe of your grain, new wine and oil, and the firstborn of your herds and flocks in the presence of the Lord your God at the place He will choose as a dwelling for His*

> *Name, so that you may learn to revere the Lord your God always."*
>
> Deuteronomy 14:22 ff.

Tithing is among the means of grace through which the New Testament believer can learn to walk with the Lord in reverential fear.

It is safe to conclude that regular tithe-giving based on the word of God is an act of reverential fear towards God.

(6) LOVE

In Luke's Gospel, the Lord Jesus rebuked the Pharisees for neglecting the love of God (Greek *agapé*). Let me quote Jesus' words verbatim:

> *"Woe to you Pharisees, because you give God a tenth of your mint, rue and all other kinds of garden herbs, but you neglect justice and the love of God. You should have practised the latter, without leaving the former undone."*
>
> Luke 11:42

Tithing without love is not only incomplete but also incorrect. God demands both at the same time. The apostle Paul, emphasizing once again the greatest gift, made the following statement to the Corinthian church:

> *"If I give all I possess to the poor and surrender my body to the flames, but have not love, I gain nothing."*
>
> 1. Corinthians 13:3

Your generosity in tithes and offerings should be released out of the knowledge of God's *agapé*. Otherwise it will profit you nothing whatsoever.

Scripture says we should love the Lord our God with all our heart, with all our soul, with all our mind and with all our strength. God's example of true love was demonstrated through the offering of His only beloved Son as a ransom for the world's sins. In your effort to honour the Lord with the tithes, offerings and substance, genuine love is required to make it acceptable in the sight of God.

(7) OBEDIENCE

Obedience is the believer's key to unlock the door to the supernatural blessings of God on his or her life. Obedience, in fact, is the whole secret of victorious living and of a successful walk with the Lord. In Deuteronomy 28:1-14, God promises to bless anyone who carefully and diligently seeks to observe and to obey His commandments.

As with love, obedience to God's revealed will must be the mindset behind every real surrender to His

Majesty. Hence, giving to God without the right spirit of obedience may in fact be recognized and adjudged by Him as a futile, fruitless exercise. Therefore, all sacrifices, offerings and tithes must be recognized as secondary to genuine, heartfelt obedience.

> *"Does the Lord delight in burnt offerings and sacrifices as much as in obeying the voice of the Lord? To obey is better than sacrifice."*
>
> 1. Samuel 15:22

Giving offerings to God is good; tithing to God is good; and sacrificing your best material possessions to Him is also good. However, sacrificing all these in true obedience is deemed to be better. May the Lord increase your obedience and return the blessing He has determined for you back into your life!

CHAPTER 16

THE ELEVEN PRINCIPAL STEPS TOWARDS SAFE TITHING

The following steps and principles will guide you into genuine tithing, acquit you from the charge of robbery, and enhance your victory over the devourer of your fruits.

Seek the place where the Lord your God chooses to put His name for His dwelling (i.e. a sound Bible believing ministry, where God's love and fear abides, and where the Lord Jesus Christ is fully and prayerfully exalted as Lord above all) and offer the tithe there (Deuteronomy 12:5 ff.).

(I) The tithe must be regarded as holy or a hallowed thing (Deuteronomy 26:13a).
(II) The tithe must be set aside (Deuteronomy 26:12).
(III) The tithe must be removed from one's house (Deuteronomy 26:13a).

(IV)   The tithe is to be given to the Levites, which, in our times, means to church ministers and elders (Deuteronomy 26:12).

(V)   Never forget to bring the tithes into the church's storehouse (Deuteronomy 26:13b).

(VI)   Do not spend the tithe on other things, even when in mourning, i.e. when in sorrow, need, or in financial difficulty, for the tithe is holy and belongs to the Lord (Deuteronomy 26:14a).

(VII) Do not subtract any of the tithe for your own pleasure and desires (Ibid.).

(VIII) Do not use the Lord's holy tithe for carnal activities, i.e. things considered dead in the sight of God (Deuteronomy 26:14b).

(IX)   Faithful tithing involves obedience: be obedient (Ibid.).

(X)   Confess your obedient act to the Lord and ask for His benediction on your life. Pray for all saints and intercede for the country in which you live.

Expect earnestly that the windows of heaven will be opened to bless you and that the devourer (seed-eater) will be rebuked for your sake according to the word of the Lord in Malachi chapter 3 verses 10 to 11.

FINAL EXHORTATION AND BENEDICTION

Exhortation

As a covenant partner, bear this in mind always: the Lord expects you to give cheerfully to the work of His kingdom without any grudge in your heart. The Scriptures say,

> *"Whoever sows sparingly will also reap sparingly, and whoever sows generously will also reap generously. Each man should give as he has decided in his heart to give, not reluctantly or under compulsion, for God loves a cheerful giver. And God is able to make all grace abound to you, so that in all things at all times, having all that you need, you will abound in every good work. As it is written: 'He has scattered abroad his gifts to the poor; his righteousness endures forever.'"*
>
> 2. Corinthians 9:6-9

Benediction

With your heart prepared, and your mind set to obey God;
I decree supernatural increase upon your life now in the authoritative, demon-expelling, poverty-removing and life-giving name of Jesus Christ.

May the power that causes a man to acquire wealth come upon you now in Jesus name.
Begin to increase; begin to expand, to the North, South, East and West.
Go beyond all boundaries and limits through the power of the Holy Spirit.
Flourish in your days, and yield your fruit in season.
Be not forsaken, and may your children never beg.
Have all good things in abundance to the glory of the Lord God, before whom you stand and whom you serve.
Now may He who supplies seed to the sower, and bread for food, supply and multiply every seed you have, and will sow in Jesus' mighty name.
Amen and Amen.

Probing Questions on, Why Be Rich?

What is your personal conviction and reason for being rich? Can you honestly answer these probing questions?

a) Do you desire to be rich? Why?

----

b) What would you choose to do first if God made you a millionaire now?

----

c) For how long would you like to maintain your wealth?

----

d) As a millionaire, what would be God's place in your life?

----

e) Would you still be faithful, if God increased the level of your finance?

----

f) Would reading the Bible every day, praying for the weak and the poor still have a meaning in your life after becoming a millionaire?

----

g) As a wealthy man/woman, how often would you give to support God's work and to assist the needy?

----

h) Supposing you do not have much now, how often have you nevertheless attempted to help the needy with the little you have?

----

i) Do you think that what you possess now is just too little for you to give some away?

----

j) How often do you help others?

----

k) Are you waiting to be rich before you can begin helping the needy, the church and the people around you?

----

l) Which kind of people would you freely like to help?

----

m) If God delayed making you rich, would you create your own way to become rich?

----

n) Can you trust God to make you wealthy?

----

o) At what age do you believe you must be wealthy?

----

p) Would you be disappointed if you failed to achieve your dream of becoming a millionaire?

----

q) Would you still love God if you saw all your companions with whom you started life prospering ahead of you?

----

r) Would you continue to be faithful in tithing if you owed the bank a lot of money?

- As a *millionaire*, how often would you tithe to God?
- As a *"thousandaire,"* how often would you tithe to God?
- As a *"hundredaire,"* would you tithe to God?
- Is God impressed by the tenth of a million Euros?
- If He is, will He not also be impressed by the tenth of a hundred Euros?
- Would you readily deny and denounce God in a severe financial crisis?
- Assuming you never became rich, would you still be content in the Lord even till death?

Your *attitude* towards answering the above questions will help determine and define your *altitude* in divine prosperity. Now, may the Lord grant you the ability needed to apply divine knowledge correctly and perfectly for lasting success.

Other books written by the author:

Stories and Epigrammatic Quotes on Tithing (82 pages)

The Four Categories of Tithers (110 pages)